The Struggle Over Eritrea, 1962–1978

Erlikh

The Struggle Over Eritrea, 1962–1978.

War and Revolution in the Horn of Africa

Haggai Erlich

HOOVER INSTITUTION PRESS
Stanford University / Stanford, California

Hoover Press Publication 260

Library of Congress Cataloging in Publication Data
Erlikh, Hagai.
   The struggle over Eritrea, 1962–1978.

   (Hoover international studies)
   Bibliography: p.
   Includes index.
   1. Eritrea (Ethiopia)—Politics and government—1962–
2. National liberation movements—Ethiopia—Eritrea.
3. Ethiopia—Politics and government—1889–1974.
4. Ethiopia—Politics and government—1974–
I. Title. II. Series.
DT397.E75 1983   963′.06   81–81169
ISBN 0–8179–7602–7

In memory of my best friends

Gideon Cosma

Alexander Gur-Arye

Oded Hermoni

who fell for peace, October 1973

Contents

Editor's Foreword

"Eritreans are Ethiopians," writes Robert Hess, a leading U.S. scholar concerned with the Horn of Africa, in his *Ethiopia: Modernization of Autocracy* (Ithaca, N.Y.: Cornell University Press, 1970). His view is shared by a variety of men and women who otherwise have little in common—surviving members of the late Emperor Haile Selassie's entourage now in exile, militant Marxist-Leninist scholars, Ethiopian field officers currently serving in Eritrea, professional Soviet agitprop representatives, and a substantial number of Eritrean Christians. English-speaking scholars in the past have taken surprisingly little interest in the Eritrean question, and the literature in that language is sparse. Stephen Hemsley Longrigg, *A Short History of Eritrea* (Oxford: Clarendon Press, 1945), reflects the writer's preoccupation as a British soldier, colonial civil servant, and chief administrator in Eritrea during the World War II British military occupation. Estelle Sylvia Pankhurst, *Eritrea on the Eve . . .* (Woodford Green, Eng.: New Times and Ethiopian News Books, 1952), mirrors that author's progressive commitments, which strangely blend the ideals of British suffragettes and Labour Party supporters with a sense of Ethiopian patriotism. Gerald K. N. Trevaskis, *Eritrea: A Colony in Transition* (London: Oxford University Press, 1960), still merits study, but is now dated and bears the marks of the decolonization era.

Haggai Erlich's work, written from the perspective of an Israeli scholar, represents a new departure for Eritrean studies in the United States. The writer has consulted a vast range of sources not accessible to the average U.S. student. His work makes a major contribution to the history of Eritrean separatism during the 1960s, the Ethiopian response, and the complex interplay of competing nationalisms. Erlich sees the Eritrean-Ethiopian struggle as a war between two competing revolutions. The Eritrean nationalists aimed not merely at separation but at a profound transformation of their country's society. Christian Tigreans, previously outnumbered by Muslims, acquired far-reaching influence. The political power of urban intellectuals began to exceed the might of tribal warriors. Field commanders gained at the expense of political leaders in exile. Gradually the Pan-Arab and mildly socialist terminology was abandoned in favor of a militant variety of Marxism, much to the distress of Eritrea's supporters in Arab countries. As Erlich sees it, Eritrean Marxism, however, remained too shallow in its roots for success. The rebels failed to develop an all-encompassing sense of Eritrean nationalism capable of unifying a country divided by regional, ethnic, and religious cleavages.

For a brief moment, victory seemed to be in the Eritreans' grasp. But according to Erlich, Col. Mangistu Haila-Mariam's victory in 1977 doomed their cause. The Ethiopians carried out a revolution of their own; they mobilized the peasant masses into a new army; they defeated the dual threats to Ethiopian unity that had arisen from Eritrea and Somalia. In Erlich's view, Soviet and Cuban aid facilitated the Ethiopian victory, but the Soviet role should not be overestimated. The Ethiopian rally was only one of the many instances in which Ethiopia—faced with disaster and national disintegration—united behind a strong ruler to ward off perils to its existence. As Erlich interprets the situation, Mangistu, in the latter part of the twentieth century, played the same role assumed by Emperors Yohannes and Menelik in face of the European threat at the end of the nineteenth century. Or—an Ethiopian might add—Mangistu, in calling on the Soviets and Cubans with their helicopters and tanks, did no more than Emperor Galawdewos, who, in the sixteenth century, restored Ethiopia's position against a Muslim attack by calling for aid from Portuguese soldiers armed with superior muskets. The Eritreans, in Erlich's interpretation, had their chance; it will not come again. Ethiopia, once secure, will play a constructive role in the Horn of Africa. Sooner or later, relations between Ethiopia and the Soviet Union will deteriorate. The West can do no better than to join the major Red Sea littoral states (Saudi Arabia, Egypt, Sudan) to lure Ethiopia out of the Soviet camp.

Such is Erlich's interpretation, argued with a wealth of detail and profound knowledge of the area. Not all scholars will agree with his assumptions. Ethiopia, a multinational empire with large Muslim and animist components, seems unstable. Its economic problems are staggering. The Soviets and Cubans appear much better entrenched in Ethiopia today than the Portuguese were four hundred years ago. The Eritrean cause, which seems likely to endure, may benefit from an unexpected turn of events. Nevertheless, Erlich's work is a major contribution to the study of Eritrea and its neighbors. As a study of the Eritrean revolution, it should stand for many years to come.

RICHARD F. STAAR

Director of International Studies
Hoover Institution

Preface

My objective in writing this book is to describe and analyze the political and military struggle over Eritrea between 1962 and 1978, a period that starts with Eritrea's reannexation to Ethiopia, culminates with the emergence of a strong nationalist movement made up of several organizations all striving to fulfill Eritrean nationalism, and ends with the struggle being decided, perhaps contrary to the expectations of many observers, in favor of Ethiopia.

I started studying the history of the region in 1970, as a doctoral student at the School of Oriental and African Studies, London University. The findings of my initial research into the late nineteenth century struggle for Eritrea involving Ethiopia, local Eritrean factors, Sudanese Mahdism, and Italian imperialism are described in my book *Ethiopia and Eritrea During the Scramble for Africa: A Political Biography of Ras Alula*. (Tel Aviv: Tel Aviv University, Shiloah Center; East Lansing: Michigan State University Press, 1982).

In studying the contemporary struggle, I was surprised to discover its comparative complexity. The main local participants—the various groups and sectors comprising the region's highly diverse society—remained the same, but increased Western and Middle Eastern involvement in the twentieth century encouraged intensive politicization and added a modern ideological dimension to old rivalries. Modern nationalistic and revolutionary ideas, as progressive as they may justifiably be regarded, considerably aggravated centuries-old local tensions and problems. But, as we shall see, tenacious traditional patterns of political organization and behavior among the struggling factors, and not the newly introduced concepts, were to determine the outcome of the struggle.

Factual reconstruction of this complex conflict and internal developments within the rival camps was not easy. Gathering the material was in itself a painstaking process, but I have tried to present the story as fully and objectively as possible. My main sources were publications of the various parties involved, as well as those of Middle Eastern, African, and Western observers. I derived invaluable information from dozens of interviews and discussions with persons directly involved in shaping these events at various stages. Even though I cannot name all my sources in the text, I take pleasure in thanking them again.

I should also like to express my gratitude to the Ford Foundation, which, through its Israel Foundation Trustees, was my major benefactor. Without its assistance, this research would simply not have materialized. Thanks for financial and other support are also due to Tel Aviv University's Shiloah Center for Middle Eastern and African Studies (headed by Prof. Itamar Rabinovitch), and especially its publication program on Africa, and the Arann School of History, and the Faculty of Humanities (notably my teacher and friend Prof. Zvi Yavetz).

The manuscript was read at different stages by my friend Prof. Howard Kushner and by experts on the contemporary Horn of Africa, such as Dr. Paul Henze of the U.S. National Security Council and Patrick Gilkes of the BBC. They all offered constructive criticism and invaluable new information for which I thank them most heartily. Clearly, however, the responsibility for any mistakes or misrepresentations is exclusively mine.

It is also my privilege to thank cordially the staff of the Hoover Institution, notably Associate Director Richard T. Burress, Ms. Phyllis Cairns, and Mr. John Ziemer, for being so kind and helpful in seeing my manuscript through publication. I am particularly grateful to Connie Wilsack for coping with my English and for her most able assistance in editing this complex story.

Finally, it is my privilege to thank my wife Hanna—for everything.

Acronyms

ALF	Afar Liberation Front
EDU	Ethiopian Democratic Union
ELF-PLF	Eritrean Liberation Front–Popular Liberation Forces
ELF-RC	Eritrean Liberation Front–Revolutionary Council
EPLF	Eritrean People's Liberation Front/Forces
EPRA	Ethiopian People's Revolutionary Army
EPRP	Ethiopian People's Revolutionary Party
LPP	Liberal Progressive Party
ML	Muslim League
Mueson	All-Ethiopian Socialist Movement
OAU	Organization of African Unity
PDRY	People's Democratic Republic of Yemen
PLF	Popular Liberation Front
PLO	Palestine Liberation Organization
PMAC	Provisional Military Administrative Council
POMOA	Political Office of Mass Organizational Affairs
TPLF	Tigrean People's Liberation Front
UAR	United Arab Republic
UP	Unionist Party
WSLF	Western Somali Liberation Forces

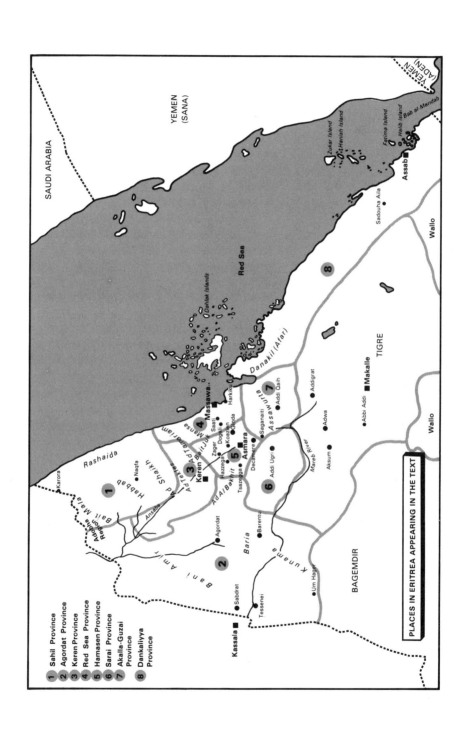

PLACES IN ERITREA APPEARING IN THE TEXT

1 Sahil Province
2 Agordat Province
3 Keren Province
4 Red Sea Province
5 Hamasen Province
6 Sarai Province
7 Akalla-Guzai Province
8 Dankaliyya Province

SAUDI ARABIA

YEMEN (SANA)

YEMEN (ADEN)

Red Sea

Bab al Mandab
Helib Island
Fatima Island
Hanish Island
Zukar Island

Assab

Dahlak Islands

Danakil (Afar)

Sadouha Aila

Wallo

TIGRE

Wallo

BAGEMDIR

Massawa
Harkiko
Saati
Dogolia
Zager
Ghinda
Manse
Koatien
Hazzega
Tsazega
Asmara
Decamere
Addi Ugri
Saganairti
Addi Qaih
Addigrat
Adwa
Aksum
Mareb River
Abbi Addi
Makalle

Keren Baitt Juk
Habbab
Naqfa
Karora

Rashaida

Bani Amir

Agordat

Baria
Barentu

Kunama
Um Hagr

Sabdrat
Tessenei

Kassala

1. Eritreans and Eritreanism

Eritrea was a problem that became a conflict, a conflict that became a local tragedy, and a local tragedy that became a pivotal issue in a regional crisis. This regional crisis gained global strategic importance. Yet the initial problem was never resolved; on the contrary, it worsened over time.

The essential problem was a matter of identity. Eritrea was reunited to Ethiopia only in 1962, after enjoying a separate history and identity for nearly seventy years. The reunification was far from a success. The Ethiopian government failed to cope constructively with local problems, and the consequent discontent was fertile ground for foreign interference. By the early 1970s, a sense of Eritrean awareness created during the twentieth-century interlude of independence had given birth to a nationalist movement and to organizations capable of fighting for the political fulfillment of Eritreanism.

The Birth of Eritrea

Eritrea, like many territorial entities of late nineteenth century Africa (with the notable exception of Ethiopia), was an artificial creation of European imperialism. The Italians, frustrated latecomers to the glories of colonialism, landed in Massawa in 1885. After a long and complicated conflict with Ethiopian Emperor Yohannes IV (1872–1889) and his general in Asmara, *Ras* Alula, they managed to occupy the territories between the Red Sea and the Mareb River. On 1 January 1890, they proclaimed their new colony, calling it

Eritrea after the Latin name for the neighboring Red Sea, Mare Erythraeum. Within four years, the Italians had expanded their colony westward and northward to include vast Muslim-populated areas. Although defeated at Adwa in March 1896 by Yohannes's successor, the Amhara-Shoan Menelik II (1889–1913), when they attempted to expand further at Ethiopia's expense, in October of the same year they obtained Menelik's full recognition of Eritrea as part of the Italian empire. Thus Eritrea, like many entities in the surrounding regions, came into being not as the political fulfillment of local nationalism but as the result of the imposition by a foreign government of its administration over a motley collection of diverse ethnic, linguistic, regional, and religious sectors.

The various elements constituting what may now be called Eritrean society reflected the highly diverse nature of the population in the Horn of Africa in general, an area whose location and natural features had long made it a meeting place for many peoples. For the purpose of discussing political developments, Eritrea may be divided in the following ways.[1]

Geographic Differences

1. *The Central Highlands.*   This core area is centered on Eritrea's capital, Asmara, and its environs and comprises about a quarter of Eritrea's territory and about half of its population. The majority of the inhabitants are Tigrinya-speaking Christians, but there is also a significant Muslim population, both peasants and town dwellers.

2. *The Southern Coastal Area.*   This area extends southward from Massawa. It is mainly a desert and contains one-fifth of the territory and one-tenth of the population; the overwhelming majority are Muslim (mostly nomads, but some peasants).

3. *The Sahil, Northern Eritrea.*   This area includes the northern coastal strip along the Red Sea and the regions lying between it and the Sudanese border. It is inhabited mostly by Tigre-speaking Muslim nomads.

4. *The Western Plateau.*   This region lies between the Gash and Setit rivers and is inhabited by Muslims (with some Christians and animists).

Ethnolinguistic Differences

1. *Tigrinya Speakers.*   Tigrinya, a Semitic language, is spoken by the inhabitants of the highlands (the districts of Hamasen, Sarai, and Akalla-Guzai), Keren, and Massawa. It is also spoken in the province of Tigre in Ethiopia proper. According to British estimates made in 1952, the number of Tigrinya speakers in Eritrea was 524,000—some 487,000 Christians and the rest Muslims.

2. *Tigre Speakers.*   The Tigre language (not to be confused with the Ethiopian province of Tigre or the Tigrinya language) is spoken by the majority of the inhabitants of the Sahil and the western plateau—members of

the Bani Amir tribes and the various Sahil clans, as well as urban dwellers and others. In 1952 the number of Tigre speakers was estimated at 329,000, of whom 322,000 were Muslims.

3. *Afar and Saho Speakers.*   These languages are spoken by members of the Afar clans, the Assawurta, and other Muslims, estimated to number 99,000 in 1952.

4. *Arabic Speakers.*   The number of Arabs in Eritrea is small, and all are concentrated in the coastal towns. Many Muslims speak and write Arabic due to the influence of Islam in the modern period.

5. *Amharic Speakers.*   Many Eritreans use Amharic because of the Ethiopian policy of Amharization following the 1962 annexation.

6. *Other Groups.*   This includes several small communities, including the Baria and Kunama, the Belain clans, and others, estimated in 1952 to number 79,000—58,000 Muslims, 14,000 Christians, and 7,000 Kunama animists.

Religious Differences

1. *Christians.*   The majority of the highlanders and some western Eritrean tribesmen are Ethiopian Christians. There are also Protestant and Catholic communities, mainly in the highland towns. They were estimated in 1952 to total 510,000, of whom 35,000 were Catholics and 16,000 were Protestants.

2. *Muslims.*   Almost all the clans and town dwellers of the coast, the Sahil, and the west and many villagers and town dwellers of the highlands are Muslims. Total estimate for 1952 was 514,000.

The Italian Period, 1890–1941

The Italian colony of Eritrea existed until the middle of World War II. However, the Italian dream of colonization by channeling Italian emigration to Eritrea instead of to the United States never materialized. At the same time, Eritrea proved to be too poor in resources to be of much economic worth. Its importance continued to lie, as from the outset, in its being a source of pride to Italian imperialist sentiment and a basis for further expansion. It was from Eritrea that in October 1935 Mussolini launched his campaign to conquer Ethiopia, a campaign that ended seven months later with the fall of Addis Ababa and Haile Selassie's exile. In 1941, however, the British conquered Africa–Orientale Italiana, reinstalled Haile Selassie, and occupied Eritrea, terminating a 51-year period of colonial rule.[2]

Italy's impact on Eritrean society was minimal; the Italians' only real concern was to make Eritrea a strong military base that could serve as a strategic springboard for expansion. They therefore constructed an impressive road and railway network and developed urban centers, but this was virtually the limit of their activity as an imperialist power. They were not interested in development per se. Although they contributed to the maintenance of law and order, subsidized the economy, and promoted health care, the tribal system of the Muslim nomads with its feudal undertones and political overtones remained largely intact. The members of the great families and regional warlords, who had led the Christian community, were, however, deprived of their political leadership, and leading personalities were reduced, at best, to the status of low-ranking bureaucrats.[3]

On the whole, the period of Italian rule contributed by its very length to the strengthening of Eritrean awareness, especially among those who underwent urbanization or served in the bureaucracy and army, although the Italians did very little to promote internal social cohesion. In fact, mostly in the context of their propaganda warfare against the British in the neighboring Middle East, they encouraged Islam and Arabic. Moreover, the church was damaged, primarily because of land confiscations, while the self-awareness of Tigrinya speakers and Tigrean sectarianism were encouraged. This was especially the case during the occupation of Ethiopia, when the neighboring province of Tigre was annexed to Eritrea (1936–1941). Yet because of the Italians' undisputed dominance, their rule was relatively free of internal political, social, and economic tensions. Its significance from today's perspective lay essentially in the existence of Eritrea as a separate entity and the preservation and even promotion of its internal diversity.

The British Period, 1941–1952

Under the British military administration, Eritrean society underwent a rapid and intensive process of politicization.[4] The British occupation was, by definition, temporary; the political future of the ex–Italian colony was to be decided by the parties concerned, including the Eritreans. Conflicting ideas and interests promoted Eritrea's political awareness and the formation of political groupings.

The British military administrators encouraged politicization, for they hoped to channel the process and promote British interests in the area. Facing instability in their Middle East bases and given Haile Selassie's new orientation toward the United States, the British conceived the Sudan as their most solid asset in the region. The British even considered dismembering Eritrea and annexing its western regions to the Sudan. British administrators gave special attention to those regions, encouraging Islam and the learning of Arabic, even bringing books from Egypt for this purpose. They also encouraged Tigreanism through the promotion of Tigrinya and through relations with the neighboring Ethiopian province of Tigre. Even as late as the end of the 1940s, important British policymakers and local administrators toyed with the idea of creating a British-influenced and British-protected Tigrean entity federated with Ethiopia.[5] Consequently, a free Eritrean press was allowed (and even subsidized), as was free political organization.

An economic crisis contributed to the politicization process. Despite British efforts, the price of basic commodities grew sixfold between 1940 and 1944, while salaries increased by only 60 percent. The end of the Italian buildup and the later exodus of Italians resulted in both urban unemployment and inflation. Under the British, Eritrean workers were allowed to unionize, and they formed a syndicate numbering 3,500–5,000 members. In the western and coastal regions, Muslim nomads and villagers were encouraged to organize against their previously Italian-supported chiefs and feudal lords. The bureaucracy was gradually Eritreanized, as both old leaders and members of a new generation were promoted to positions of administrative responsibility.

Other external factors contributed to the process of politicization. Many Italian policymakers tried to promote the idea of Italian trusteeship over the ex-colony. More effectively, Emperor Haile Selassie, once back on his throne, started working relentlessly for the restoration of Eritrea to Ethiopia, his emissaries joining hands with the Eritrean priesthood in an effort to organize supporters of reunification politically.

The British-initiated politicization of Eritrean society was effective primarily in unleashing uncontrollable forces. Desiring to promote Great Britain's strategic interests, the British encouraged political activity without regard for the extreme fragmentation of Eritrean society and without taking precautions to channel it in ways that would reduce the possibility of irreconcilable clashes.

This intensive process of politicization did not, however, stimulate an Eritrean nationalist movement. In the 1940s, the Eritrean intelligentsia was still too small and too isolated to be influenced by nationalist struggles in the neighboring Middle East. Whatever Eritrean self-awareness existed was apparently too weak to overcome the old and now encouraged sectarian differences. In fact, only a slight majority at best of politically active Eritreans were for independence, and many of them favored some sort of a trusteeship regime. The overwhelming majority of Christian Tigreans (the main inhabitants of the core highlands) wanted reunification with Ethiopia. Indeed, rather than encouraging the emergence of Eritrean nationalism (which was not to emerge as a significant movement until the 1970s), processes at work in the 1940s resulted in the politicization of Eritrean ethnic, religious, and regional diversity. A further catalyst in this process was visits by various U.N. commissions charged with assessing the situation in the ex-colony in order to decide Eritrea's future.

Political parties and organizations expressing the interests of various sectors were established, and most of them remained active throughout the period.[6] The Unionist Party (UP), which advocated reunification with Ethiopia under Haile Selassie as an act of national liberation, consisted primarily of Christian highlanders and some Muslims. Most members of the Muslim League (ML), were Muslim advocates of independence. (After the establishment of another party named the National Muslim Party of Massawa, the ML represented mainly the Muslims of western Eritrea.) The Liberal Progressive Party (LPP) comprised Christians and some Muslims advocating independence, preferably with the annexation of Tigre province to Eritrea. Although Eritrean Christians were Tigrinya speakers, only a tiny minority raised the issue of Tigreanism in the 1940s. The majority conceived Haile Selassie as a national hero, even though he was then working to end the semiautonomy of Tigre province. Finally there were the new Eritrean Pro-Italy Party, composed of many half-castes, and a number of other minor parties. In 1948–1949 the Muslim-dominated parties and the majority of the LPP joined forces to form the Independence Bloc. This organization soon split up, with some factions joining the UP and others forming new parties, including the Muslim League of the Western Province, the Eritrean Democratic Bloc, the Independent Muslim League, and the renewed LPP.

Depoliticization in Ethiopia

While Eritrean society was undergoing intensive politicization, neighboring Ethiopia was experiencing the opposite: rapid centralization of power and the depoliticization of society.

When Haile Selassie returned to power in 1941, he found himself in a better position than his predecessors had been to realize the medieval Ethiopian concept of absolute emperorship. Ethiopia was the only civilization and political entity in Africa and the Middle East to withstand the aggressive challenge of Europe in the late nineteenth century and to emerge from the clash with Western imperialism with a strong sense of national pride. The general result was that Ethiopian political and social values remained oriented toward the past. They had been proven valid; there was thus no need (at least in the eyes of the ruling classes) to revolutionize concepts and systems. On the contrary, in the early twentieth century, "modernization" meant the cautious borrowing of European administrative and technological achievements in order to further entrench the old political institutions and concepts. The defeat by the Italians in the mid-1930s and the ensuing five-year period of fascist imperialism in Ethiopia changed very little in this respect. In fact, paradoxically, it later helped Haile Selassie to implement imperial absolutism, for the period of occupation was too short and the Ethiopian intelligentsia too few to enable the mostly provincial and uncoordinated resistance movement to develop into an alternative political leadership. At the same time, the fascists quite efficiently destroyed the military might of the provincial warlords. Back in Addis Ababa in 1941, Haile Selassie could safely start modernizing the educational system and the army in order to build a modern military and bureaucratic structure in the service of imperial centralism.

But although the old decentralized political structure was eliminated, the process of centralization was not accompanied by political modernization. Modern political concepts and institutions adopted in the neighboring countries, including Eritrea, were rejected. Imperial absolutism, as traditionally conceived, continued to grow throughout the 1940s and 1950s, preventing the emergence of political movements or the public expression of new ideas. The constitutional approach borrowed from Europe, as expressed in the Ethiopian constitutions of 1931, 1955, and the like, served merely to create "constitutional absolutism." Unlike Eritrea, Ethiopia had no political parties and no free press, nor was there any institutionalized representation of popular interests. Instead, a modern state machinery, based on Western-educated bureaucrats and a Western-trained army, was built to assert the control of a politically medieval emperorship all over the country.

By the 1950s, Ethiopia's diverse ethnic, religious, regional, and linguistic groups had been almost completely depoliticized. The old elite and educated youngsters, integrating into the state machinery, tended more and more to identify with Ethiopian statehood.

From Federation to Annexation, 1952–1962

It was at this stage in their history that politically centralized Ethiopia and politically pluralist Eritrea were federated. Between 1947 and 1951, the future of Eritrea was debated in the forums of international diplomacy. The diplomatic struggle over the ex-colony influenced internal developments in Eritrea, but the details are outside the scope of this background to the later story of 1962–1978.[7] At the end of the process, however, there emerged among the Great Powers and in the United Nations a compromise based essentially on Ethiopia's historical rights and economic and strategic needs, and the U.N. General Assembly adopted the idea of a federation in December 1950. On 15 September 1952, the British flag was lowered from the Government House in Asmara and the federation came into being. It remained in existence for ten years, a period characterized by an uneven contest between Ethiopia's imperial absolutism and Eritrea's political pluralism.[8]

In retrospect it is clear that the federation was doomed because of the nature of the Ethiopian political system. First, absolute emperorship could hardly coexist with political pluralism. Second, Ethiopia was even more diverse than Eritrea in terms of ethnic, linguistic, religious, and regional groups; Eritrea's unique status would inevitably encourage the emergence of separatist movements throughout the empire. Third, the neighboring Muslim and Arab countries were gaining independence (the Sudan in January 1956), which would inevitably affect Eritrea's Muslims and fan Ethiopia's centuries-old fears of Islamic encirclement, encroachment, and penetration.

The U.N. resolution concerning the federation stipulated that "Eritrea shall constitute an autonomous unit federated with Ethiopia under the sovereignty of the Ethiopian crown." On paper, the functional structure of the federation as laid down in its constitution seemed to be clear: the federal government (in fact, the emperor) was to control foreign affairs, defense, finance, commerce, and the ports. An Eritrean executive answerable to an Eritrean assembly was to have full internal power over all functions not vested in the federal government. The initial assembly was to be elected on the basis of existing political parties.[9]

The first assembly (1952–1956), elected while Eritrea was still under British administration, contained 32 members of the UP, 18 of the Eritrean Democratic Bloc, 15 of the Muslim League of the Western Province, 1 of the Independent Muslim League, 1 of the Nationalist Party, and 1 independent member. These results showed that the U.N. formula suggesting the settlement of Eritrean politics in accord with the wishes of the majority of the population was good only in theory. In reality it was meaningless and unworkable—Eritrea's fragmented society had no majority.

In Addis Ababa the federation was conceived from the start as but a temporary obstacle on the road to full reunification. The federation arrangement and constitution were openly ignored and, in time, practically destroyed. When Haile Selassie enacted the revised 1955 constitution for his people, no mention was made of Eritrea's special status. On the contrary, the first article reasserted that "the Empire of Ethiopia comprises all the territories, including islands and the territorial waters, *under the sovereignty of the Ethiopian Crown* [italics added]. Its sovereignty and territory are indivisible."[10]

In practice, then, the federation was fictitious almost from the start. The federal government (that is, Haile Selassie's government, for a "federal government" was never established) controlled defense and finances. By taking advantage of the presence of an overwhelmingly pro-Ethiopian Christian community, it had no difficulty in taking over all positions of real power. Systematic terrorism and other measures against individuals who failed to see the light of reunification proved effective.[11] In the constitutional sphere, however, the process was more visible, and therefore much slower. The tactics pursued by the emperor in this respect were to destroy the federation through the function of his personal representative in Eritrea and to persuade the Eritrean assembly to exercise its constitutional right to vote itself out of existence.

The federal constitution defined the emperor's representative (*enderase*) in Eritrea as the link between the crown, at the head of the federation, and Eritrean institutions; but for all practical purposes, the emperor's representative was the ruler of the territory. The *enderase*'s speech to the Eritrean assembly in March 1953 left no doubts regarding his understanding of the functional structure of the federation: "There are no internal nor external affairs as far as the office of His Imperial Majesty's Representative is concerned, and there will be none in future.[12]

This approach, accompanied by a campaign of riots, left the assembly no alternative but to sanction the systematic depoliticization of Eritrean society. Well before the 1956 elections, all political parties had been banned and dismembered, with the exception of the UP, whose continued existence was permitted for propaganda reasons. Many prominent opponents of annexation had to go into exile. The trade unions were destroyed, and the press came under federal control. The office of chief executive, held until 1955 by the leader of the UP, was transferred to the representative's deputy. In December 1958 the assembly unanimously abrogated the Eritrean flag, and from September 1959 Ethiopian law was introduced. In May 1960 the assembly changed the name of the Eritrean executive to "Eritrean administration under Haile Selassie, the emperor of Ethiopia." On 15 November 1962, the assembly voted its own dissolution and Eritrea's full reunification with Ethiopia.

Ethiopia's reannexation of Eritrea must also be seen in a regional context. The late 1950s and early 1960s were marked by rising Pan-Arabism and Islamic solidarity. Nasserist revolutionary fervor swept the area. Ethiopia felt on the defensive, especially as the regime was beginning to be challenged from within (as the abortive coup d'etat of December 1960 demonstrated). In July 1960 the Republic of Somali was born. Backed by Nasser and other Arab leaders, it claimed a third of Ethiopia's territory. In September 1962, following a revolution in neighboring Yemen, the Egyptian army landed there on the pretext of Egypt's alliance with a local ally. Ethiopia had good reason for alarm since a potential local ally of Egypt was already in the making in Eritrea: the Eritrean Liberation Movement, centered in Cairo, which had been established by exiles in 1956. By the late 1950s, "the movement had organized seven-member cells in most Eritrean cities, and played a prominent role in the political mobilization of the Eritrean masses."[13] In September 1961 an open rebellion by Muslim separatists, later to adopt the name Eritrean Liberation Front (ELF), broke out in western Eritrea. In these circumstances, the political prestige Haile Selassie had gained throughout Africa during this period and the material support he received from the United States made the prophylactic annexation of Eritrea almost inevitable.

One can only speculate about the future of the federation and Eritrea's democratic regime had they not been destroyed by the Ethiopian government. Could they have survived? Is it valid to assume that Eritrea's Muslims or other social groups would not have exploited favorable regional processes in the 1950s, 1960s, and 1970s and fulfilled separatist aspirations by creating an independent Eritrean state? Could Eritrean political pluralism, built under the auspices of a European military administration, have survived full Eritrean independence? Or would it have fallen victim, as has been the case in almost all nearby countries, to the emergence of a new generation of military leaders?

These speculations must remain speculations. Eritrea was annexed to Ethiopia through the liquidation of the Eritrean political system and many symbols of self-identification. Even many of the Christian Eritreans who had favored the process at the outset started to identify Ethiopia with oppressive absolutism, while some, following the Muslims, began working actively for the fulfillment of their self-identification as Eritreans. In retrospect, this sentiment proved strong enough to motivate prolonged armed conflict.

The Emergence of Eritreanism, 1962–1974

The following chapters describe and analyze the political aspects of the ensuing conflict over Eritrea. Aspects of secondary consequence for the political situation, such as economic or social developments, receive only cursory treatment. The blowing up of one bridge by a few guerrillas may well have more immediate political importance than a ten-year effort to develop a school system. Focusing on political developments, however, blurs the background. Despite the political developments described below, Eritrea during the 1960s was, generally speaking, not such a bad place for Eritreans to live. The overwhelming majority of the population continued to enjoy politically passive, normal lives. Eritrea in the mid-1960s had a good third of the modern industrial capacity of Ethiopia. Eritrea's well-developed infrastructure combined with the strength of its large Italian community (encouraged by the imperial government to stay and lead the economic field) gave Eritrea an enormous advantage over the rest of Ethiopia. From the 1950s on, the Italians developed a significant number of new enterprises, often in cooperation with Eritreans. In fact, Eritrea was the second fastest developing region in the country after the metropolitan province of Shoa.

Another factor of considerable socioeconomic importance during the 1950s and 1960s was the growing participation of Eritreans in Ethiopian national life. Because of the higher level of education in Eritrea and the administrative experience that many young Eritreans gained during the period of British rule, Eritrea was able to supply Ethiopia with considerable manpower. Many modern organizations, such as Ethiopian Airlines, employed a disproportionate number of Eritreans. The same was true of the expanding educational system and almost every branch of Ethiopia's developing bureaucracy. The proportion of Eritreans at the university in Addis Ababa in the 1960s was higher by far than their proportion in the population. Perhaps more significant was the large number of Eritrean businessmen active in Ethiopia as a whole, as well as in Ethiopia's foreign trade and other economic relationships. Finally, Eritreans reached the highest positions in Ethiopia's government and army. Indeed, as we shall see, Ethiopia's first head of state following the deposition of Haile Selassie in 1974 was from Eritrea.

Yet, in spite of the growing participation of Eritreans in Ethiopian national life, the 1960s ended with the emergence of an Eritrean nationalist movement. The main reason why at the beginning of the decade what was little more than a Muslim separatist movement developed into a full-fledged Eritrean nationalist movement was the Ethiopian government's inflexibility and the consequent alienation of the Christian community in Eritrea. The reasons for this inflexibility, which stemmed from the very nature of the imperial regime, are outlined below.

Once Eritrean Christians joined the Muslim separatists, Eritrean nationalism was on its way. As nationalists, by their very nature, are uncompromising, the conflict became a tragedy of escalating bloodshed and war.

Ethiopianism Versus Eritreanism

When facing a situation of bloody conflict, the outside observer can hardly remain indifferent. All-too-human concern with who is right must not prejudice the carefully balanced evaluation of events; yet morally this concern cannot be laid aside.

As is often the case, history cannot provide a definite answer. The reason is simply that Eritrea did not exist prior to 1890. It was an artificial creation of the Italians, and every attempt to describe it as an entity existing prior to that date and to base historical claims on this assumption distorts the facts.[14] History merely shows that each side may claim rights to but a part of today's Eritrea. Indeed, extensive areas of Eritrea, essentially the Muslim-populated areas of western and northern Eritrea, were never (with the exception of short insignificant episodes) under the political control of Ethiopian emperors. By any objective criterion, those territories annexed to Eritrea by the Italians between 1890 and 1894 cannot historically be considered part of Ethiopia. (This observation does not contradict the otherwise valid argument that prior to European penetration of the region, the Ethiopian concept of borders and boundaries was not that of demarcated, agreed-on lines, but was based on the extent of the emperor's or his representatives' ability to exercise power, to tax, or to launch raids.)

On the other hand, the core regions of today's Eritrea (essentially, the Christian-populated central highlands) were undoubtedly an integral part—indeed, the cradle—of Ethiopian civilization, statehood, and history. The direct control of the emperors over these areas fluctuated according to their ability to exercise power in distant regions. Local rulers were always connected politically, culturally, and economically with the empire. In fact, the Eritrean highlands constituted the political and cultural core of the Ethiopian state during its first millennium (until the ninth century), when it was centered on the town of Aksum (only some 40 kilometers south of the Mareb River). During the first stage (1270–1529) of the so-called Solomonic dynasty, the majority of the emperors exercised power beyond the Mareb—some of them in person, others through local representatives.[15] This was the situation, though to a much lesser extent, throughout the sixteenth and seventeenth centuries. During the so-called Era of the Princes (ca. 1769–1855), the power of the emperors declined, and local chiefs all over Ethiopia, including the leading families beyond the Mareb, enjoyed political autonomy. (Even so, the Eritrean highlands were frequently controlled by the rulers of neighboring Tigre.) Following the renewal of imperial power at the beginning of the modern period, the Ethiopian crown reasserted direct control over the territory beyond the Mareb and over the Red Sea coast. In 1872, Tigre again became the political center of the empire with the coming to power of the Tigrean Emperor Yohannes IV (d. 1889). His general, *Ras* Alula, was put in charge of the Mareb Mellash (the Ethiopian name for the territories beyond the Mareb), which became the site of Ethiopia's successful battles against khedival Egypt (1875, 1876), Mahdist Sudan (1885), and imperialist Italy (1887).[16] Alula established the town of Asmara (1884) as his capital, centralized Eritrea's administration and economy, and asserted his control over Keren and what later became western Eritrea. As governor of Asmara, Alula gained a reputation of invincibility. It was only in late 1888, when Yohannes called him to help fight the invading Sudanese Mahdists, that the Italians were able to move inland from the coast, occupy deserted Asmara, and proceed to the Mareb River.

Thus by any historical criterion, the Eritrean highlands are an integral part of Ethiopia. The Christian-populated districts of Hamasen, Sarai, and Akalla-Guzai have historically been more a part of Ethiopia's political framework and culture than have the provinces of southern Ethiopia (Kaffa, Wallaga, Arusi, and others) occupied by Ethiopia in the late nineteenth century, which are today undisputed parts of Ethiopia.

In any case, historical facts, even if they can provide an academically satisfactory answer to a question, are seldom relevant to a living conflict. This is especially the case in the dispute between Ethiopia and Eritrea. Members of both camps have excellent reasons to believe in and fully identify with their nationalist cause. In such a situation, then, the outsider is left with the following moral criterion: the right side is the one that is aware of the rights and necessities of its rival and acts accordingly.

Unfortunately, if this is the criterion, both sides were systematically and consistently in the wrong throughout the entire period under discussion. Indeed, the central thesis of the analysis of the Eritrean conflict between 1962 and 1978 as presented here is that in both the Ethiopian and Eritrean camps, the hard-liners were gaining the upper hand in the internal struggle for leadership. Those who stood for a decisive victory through the use of military power defeated those who advocated a policy of political compromise. The dialectical dynamism of the conflict was essentially that the victory of the hard-liners in one camp played into the hands of the hard-liners in the rival camp and helped them to strengthen their position as architects of policy. Indeed, this mechanism, rather than the actual military confrontation between the two sides, was the main factor behind the constant escalation.

The Eritrean nationalist movement reflected the diversity of Eritrean society. Eritrean politics was pluralistic from the beginning, and the struggle for nationalist fulfillment was accompanied and much influenced by the internal competition for leadership between representatives of the various sectors and generations. This internal struggle was a source of both radicalism and weakness. Indeed, as will be shown, the result was political disunity, a lack of even minimal military cooperation, and civil war between the movement's different organizations, mainly the Eritrean Liberation Front–Revolutionary Council (ELF-RC) and the Eritrean People's Liberation Forces (EPLF). Moreover, the distrust and personal rivalries that separated the main leaders in effect made it impossible to obtain significant political and military support from outside sources. Thus, in 1977, internal disunity undercut what seemed to be the best chance for fulfilling Eritrean nationalist aspirations.

The Ethiopian political system, which had undergone intensive centralization in the 1950s and early 1960s, began to come apart by the early 1970s. The aging Haile Selassie became increasingly unable to take personal charge of all his empire's problems, and this led to fragmentation in policymaking. By the second half of the 1960s, at a time when the Eritrean conflict was constantly escalating, Ethiopian policymaking was largely the result of a bitter competition between rival members of Haile Selassie's establishment. A complex internal network of intrigues, jealousies, and personal ambitions developed between the empire's leading personalities in preparation for the struggle for power that would start once the old monarch was gone. The emperor himself, attempting to continue the age-old Ethiopian version of divide and rule (*shum shir*), encouraged competition and fomented rivalries.

Although this practice was not new in Ethiopia, it came to have an increasingly important impact on policymaking as the aging emperor showed a growing tendency to indulge in world affairs rather than bother about domestic problems. In this jockeying for future power, the Eritrean issue played a pivotal role; the winners were those who adopted an inflexible approach toward the Eritrean problem by advocating a military solution. The activities of these Ethiopian hard-liners contributed more than any other factor to the creation of the Eritrean nationalist movement.

Tragically for the Ethiopians, these rivalries, which intensified in the early 1970s, paralyzed the government. Thus, while the country was facing drought, famine, and inflation, its political establishment was concerned only with the political succession, while the emperor himself was blind to the developing reality. These circumstances sparked the popular protest movement that led to the 1974 revolution.

The Ethiopian revolution did not mean significant change for Eritrea. New contestants may have joined the struggle for power in Addis Ababa, but the implications for Eritrea remained the same. The new ruling body that replaced the old political establishment in Ethiopia soon became the arena for a violent contest of elimination fired by the desire for power. Once again, the Eritrean issue played a pivotal role. Once again, hard-liners advocating a military solution defeated those who favored a political solution for the problem of Eritrea.

The victory of hard-liners in both camps escalated the conflict. What was until 1974 a guerrilla war became a costly, conventional war threatening the Ethiopian state and the strategic balance in the Red Sea. Following the reopening of the Suez Canal in 1975, the Red Sea re-emerged as a main artery of the West's economy. The Soviets' presence in the region—especially their massive involvement in Ethiopia after early 1977—constituted a major threat to the Western desire for stability in the Red Sea and Persian Gulf region. Thus, as the Eritrean conflict became a conventional war, it attracted the attention and active interest of the major powers.

Revolutions at War, 1974–1978

Despite the escalation to full-scale war following the revolution in Ethiopia, the struggle over Eritrea essentially followed the old pattern— namely, the main factors were internal political developments within the two camps rather than the military clash between them. Indeed, without considering these internal developments, the story of the struggle over Eritrea between 1974 and 1978 makes no sense. By the middle of 1977, the Eritreans had gained almost every military advantage. They had captured some 90 percent of

Eritrea's territory, including the strategic town of Keren. They had twice as many trained fighters as the Ethiopians did. Organizations in Ethiopia opposed to the new government were in the process of capturing the provinces of Bagemdir and Tigre and parts of Wallo, thereby creating a buffer zone between Eritrea and central Ethiopia. The Ethiopian army, demoralized, politicized, deprived almost fully—for reasons to be discussed—of its colonels and generals, was unsuccessfully facing the massive Somali invasion of the Ogaden. Simultaneously, as if Providence were tailoring a golden opportunity for the Eritreans, an important development was occurring in the Red Sea. For the first time in modern history, the strongest Red Sea Arab states were coordinating a common Red Sea strategy. Under the indirect auspices of the United States, the Saudis, the Egyptians, and the Sudanese attempted to prevent further Soviet penetration by calling for the Arabization of the Red Sea. The establishment of an independent Eritrea led by a generation of Eritrean leaders who for two decades had been pinning their hopes on Pan-Arabism could have been an important step toward the fulfillment of this slogan. In fact, they could hardly have hoped for military and strategic circumstances more favorable to the goal of fulfilling Eritrean nationalism through the capture of the entire territory and the proclamation of an Arab-oriented independent Eritrea.

Yet the history of the conflict over Eritrea was channeled in another direction and was determined by quite different factors. While the Eritrean nationalist movement failed to exploit the favorable circumstances created by unique opportunities, Ethiopia managed to regroup, find a powerful and (for the moment) a generous ally, rebuild a much stronger army, and regain regional hegemony. By the end of 1978, Keren and almost all of Eritrea were again under Ethiopian control. Practically, the Eritreans' chance of achieving self-determination was gone.

The casual observer, unfamiliar with the history of the Horn of Africa, might assume that Ethiopia's recovery and victory can be attributed solely to massive Soviet aid. Though important, this factor must be seen in proper perspective. Soviet arms and aid facilitated the process, they did not create it. Equally, it was not the lack of arms and strong allies that led the Eritreans to disunity, isolation, and defeat. The real story of the conflict was not merely a series of clashes between armies; the main point was that each political community, each nationalism, was simultaneously undergoing an internal revolution.

In the mid-1970s, both Ethiopia and the Eritrean nationalist movement were experiencing a profound and significant revolution. But while Ethiopian nationalism and statehood were strong enough to survive and even benefit from very painful revolutionary surgery, the historically rootless Eritrean society and Eritrean nationalist movement were too fragmented to survive a similar trial. More specifically, after three years of confusion and anarchy, the internal political process in Ethiopia that started with the revolution ended with the victory of the wing whose slogan was "Unity or Death." In the Eritrean movement in contrast, the faction that emerged as the stronger following the internal revolution advocated "Revolution before Unity." The combined effect of these processes led one camp to victory and the other to defeat. For many casual observers, the Eritrean defeat was a most surprising development. For a persistent student of the region, the recovery of Ethiopian nationalism and statehood and the inability of the Eritreans to unite under a centralized leadership was quite compatible with historical patterns.

That Ethiopia has been undergoing a revolution since 1974 needs no elaboration. For this discussion, however, it is important to refer to one related aspect—namely, the implications of the revolution for Ethiopia's ability to maintain its integrity. From this point of view, it is apparent that in the short run, the 1974 revolution was destructive. It resulted in the eradication of the existing political establishment, severe erosion of the state machinery, and politicization of the armed forces. Essentially, the events of 1974 in Addis Ababa stemmed from the unexpected success of a spontaneous protest movement rather than from planned revolutionary change. In destroying the old order, the revolutionaries damaged the military and bureaucratic foundations of the state severely, but failed to provide proper substitutes. The constant bloody struggles from 1974 to 1977 within the new ruling body (the Derg) and among the many new groups and underground movements reflected the fragmentation of the political system and differences of opinion over basic questions facing the disintegrating state, particularly the question of Eritrea. The intensification of these internal conflicts, together with the strengthening of various separatist movements, created the impression that Ethiopian statehood and nationalism would be unable to withstand the trials of the continuing revolution.

During the same period, the Eritrean nationalist movement also underwent a revolution. Since Eritrean nationalists have always referred to their movement as a revolutionary one, the occurrence of a *real* revolution within their ranks escaped the eyes of most observers. However, the Eritrean movement changed profoundly, both quantitatively and qualitatively, between 1975 and 1977.

From the quantitative point of view, this period was one of rapid and significant growth in membership. Up to 1974 the number of active Eritrean fighters was estimated at no more than 2,500. Following the revolution in Ethiopia and for other related reasons, the Eritrean camps started to swell. In early 1975 the number of organized Eritrean fighters was estimated at 6,000. By early 1977 estimates varied from 38,500 to 43,000.

At the same time, the Eritrean movement was experiencing significant qualitative changes. For example, Christian Tigreans, previously grossly outnumbered by Muslims, started dominating the strongest Eritrean organization, the EPLF. The political weight of members of the urban intelligentsia began to exceed that of tribal warriors. Field commanders gained influence at the expense of leaders in exile and finally displaced them completely. In both the EPLF and the ELF-RC, cadres in the field, representing views expressed in mass meetings of fighters, came to control the supreme commands. Correspondingly, the Eritrean movement underwent a fundamental ideological change. The two leading organizations abandoned Pan-Arabist and mildly socialist terminology in favor of Marxist and radical revolutionary phraseology.

In short, the revolution in the Eritrean movement stemmed both from growth and from qualitative improvement. The immediate impact of the Ethiopian revolution on national unity and military ability was debilitating. No wonder that the Eritreans, abandoning guerrilla tactics for full-scale conventional warfare, gained repeated successes. But this state of affairs did not last long. While Ethiopian nationalism, statehood, and society proved strong enough to survive such a revolution, Eritreanism proved too weak to stand the trial of growing radicalism and revolutionism.

In both Ethiopia and the Eritrean movement, revolution intensified the internal struggles for power. In Addis Ababa the struggle for power became a brutal and gory one—a process of elimination in the starkest sense. As in the period before the revolution, the escalating situation in Eritrea helped the hard-liners in this internal game, and it was Lt. Col. Mangistu Haila-Mariam, the head of the faction advocating the restoration of centralized authority in Ethiopia, who emerged victorious in early 1977. In practical terms, Mangistu's policy of "Unity or Death" meant according priority to whatever served the interests of centralism and the state's integrity. Mangistu's main rivals in this struggle for power, military and civilian alike (with the notable exception of Lt. Gen. Aman Andom, the first head of state after the fall of the emperor), were inclined to promote the revolution at the expense of centralism.

Whatever one may think of Mangistu's personality and merciless methods, his victory in the internal struggle for power was a victory over the fragmentation caused by the tumultuous events of 1974. Moreover, Mangistu's emergence as the undisputed ruler of the Derg followed a pattern often seen in Ethiopia's long history. Facing an external threat, Ethiopian society has on many occasions regrouped under the leadership of an ambitious individual. The most obvious example was the reunification of Ethiopia by the Emperors Yohannes and Menelik in the face of the late nineteenth century European imperialist threat. An explanation of this phenomenon would require a discussion of Ethiopian sociopolitics outside the scope of this analysis; here it is sufficient to argue that Soviet and Cuban aid, though contributing to and facilitating this process of national regrouping, did not create it. Facing their moment of truth, the Ethiopians' social structure and values and their strong national and political tradition enabled a charismatic personality to assert leadership. Revolutionary phraseology, now irrelevant, was put aside.

It was, indeed, under the traditional nationalist slogan of "Our Mother, Ethiopia" and the Cross and St. George that Ethiopia mobilized its new national army. This large army was the force that defeated (with the active help of Cubans and Soviets) Ethiopia's external enemies; its rebuilding was an important step in the reconstruction of Ethiopia's state machinery. Significantly, this army consisted essentially of peasants recruited from the provinces, not the indoctrinated students or the pro-revolution urban intelligentsia who had helped in creating the 1974 revolution.

In Eritrea, as in Ethiopia, the revolution intensified the struggle for leadership and power, but unlike the Ethiopians, the Eritreans, replete with the successes they had enjoyed in 1975–1977, abstained from fighting each other. Yet, the main process in the Eritrean movement was the victory of radical revolutionism over the Eritrean nationalist interest. In essence, the political game within the Eritrean movement resulted in the victory of pro-revolution, Marxist-oriented cadres in the field over the old guard of Pan-Arabist and mildly socialist leaders in exile. At the same time, the more radical EPLF gained ascendance over the ELF-RC as the strongest but definitely not the dominant factor in the movement, and a third organization, the Eritrean Liberation Front–Popular Liberation Forces (ELF-PLF), came into being. A united Eritrean nationalist leadership did not emerge during this period— quite the opposite.

In the struggle among these different factors, revolutionary phraseology served to legitimize the old and now reinforced disunity and to foment mutual distrust. With the Ethiopian army shattered and besieged, many Eritreans seemed to take victory for granted. The more radical EPLF saw immediate unity as a compromise on both the organization of future government and revolutionism. Though it was not said in so many words, the EPLF placed revolution before unity. Leaders advocating national unity as a precondition to victory, like some of the prominent commanders of the ELF-RC (and Uthman Salih Sabi of the ELF-PLF), were seen as reactionaries and counter-revolutionaries.

Against the background of deep-rooted Eritrean sectarianism, all efforts to establish some sort of unity proved fruitless. Unlike the Ethiopians, the Eritreans had no unifying nationalist tradition to help them, nor did they enjoy a sociopolitical mechanism enabling the emergence of an all-Eritrean leader. Eritreanism, a very young emotion, was essentially the negation of

Ethiopianism rather than a historically rooted supratribal, supralinguistic, and suprareligious sense of Eritrean affiliation. Lacking such slogans as "Our Mother, Eritrea," the Eritrean nationalists remained the captives of sectarian interests that they justified with borrowed ideologies. (Not only the newly adopted radical Marxism but also the now abandoned Pan-Arabism had little to do with Eritrean ethnic, cultural, or historical reality.) Failing to unite in 1977 when victory seemed imminent, the Eritreans also failed to unite later in defeat.

The victory of revolutionism over the Eritrean nationalist interest resulted not only in disunity but also in regional isolation. As already mentioned, 1976 and 1977 saw the creation of a strong Red Sea Arab front. The anti-Soviet Riyadh-Cairo-Khartoum axis promoted the Arabization of the Red Sea. The establishment of a moderate Arab-oriented Eritrea could have been the culmination of such a regional strategy. Indeed—as we shall see—the old guard of Eritrean leaders had yearned for two decades for such a situation. Their dream was now a reality, and at the same time as Ethiopia was weakening and the strength of the Eritrean organizations was growing. Yet because of the Eritrean revolution and the victory of radical Marxism over Pan-Arabism, it became impossible to realize the opportunity latent in this combination of favorable circumstances. The rich and influential Saudis saw Uthman Salih Sabi and other veterans as their partners in a regional strategy, but these leaders came to be replaced by young Marxists, especially from the EPLF. The EPLF, vocal advocates not only of revolution in Eritrea but in the region as a whole, were seen in Riyadh and other Arab capitals as the nucleus of a future Aden-type locus of instability. In these circumstances, to aid the EPLF, and to a slightly lesser extent the ELF-RC, was to promote radicalism rather than Pan-Arabism. When the Eritrean movement's erstwhile supporters—the pro-Soviet radicals in Libya and South Yemen—started supporting Ethiopia, the Eritreans, captives of their revolutionary phraseology, failed to make new allies. They were thus led by disunity to radicalism, and by radicalism to isolation and defeat.

A comparison of the terminology and phraseology used by the revolutionaries of both Ethiopia and Eritrea proves that from the ideological point of view, the two revolutions were similar. For example, the Derg's National Democratic Revolution Program of May 1976 and the resolutions of the EPLF congress of January 1977 are identical in substance.

Such a comparison, however, is fruitless. What is relevant and practical is to examine phenomena like revolutions and nationalist struggles in the light of social, political, and military reality. In the case considered here, ideologically similar revolutions developing in the context of the same conflict resulted in one nation rebuilding its broken power and the other losing its best chance for national independence. Ethiopia's recovery and victory cannot be understood without studying Ethiopia's long past as a civilization, state, and nation, a task obviously beyond the scope of the present work. Only against such a background is it possible to explain Ethiopia's ability to unite under the leadership of an ambitious individual at a time of external pressure and internal stress.

Equally, one cannot understand the Eritrean failure without knowing the history and reality of Eritrean society. Only against this background can the failure of Eritrean society to mobilize itself behind a united leadership be understood. In the absence of such leadership, despite two decades of fighting for self-determination, the Eritreans are still only a nation in the making.

As we have seen in this brief introductory review, Eritrean nationalism, a by-product of recent history, is based essentially on the negation of Ethiopianism. Prior to the Eritreans' bitter experiences with Ethiopian authorities, an all-Eritrean sentiment barely existed. Today, although this sentiment is unquestionably strong, the Eritreans have yet to prove themselves able to build an all-Eritrean movement. Their young nationalism, however sincere, is apparently still too shallow and rootless to help Eritreans overcome a historically rooted sectarianism and the temptations of destructive radicalism.

Ethiopian nationalism, in contrast, stems from twenty centuries of flexible and pragmatic continuity. Throughout their long history, the Ethiopians have proved able to enrich their national tradition by incorporating imported ideas selectively. Will they now succeed in avoiding the temptations of borrowed radicalism and build their revolution on the solid ground of Ethiopianism? The answer to this question, though partially given by the story told in the following chapters, is not yet clear.

2. The Eritrean Separatists, 1962–1973

Until 1967, the young Eritrean separatist movement, still relatively small, was free of internal conflicts. This stemmed not from harmonious coexistence between the movement's various sectors, but from the lack of intensive common activity.

The period was still under the shadow of the act of annexation. The unilateral cancellation of the symbols of Eritrean uniqueness and the brutality of Ethiopian authorities in dealing with those who opposed this step constructed a bridge of understanding between the two major sectors of the Eritrean movement—the exiles based in Arab capitals, who had been members of the Eritrean political leadership during the British military administration (1941–1952), and the Eritreans who resisted the Ethiopians in the field. (At the beginning of this period, these were almost exclusively Muslims, primarily members of the Bani Amir tribes and clans of western Eritrea and the coastal zones.) The leaders in exile thus bestowed on the armed groups of irregular warriors led by tribal leaders the image and the legitimacy of an organized nationalist freedom movement.

On 1 September 1961, Hamid Idris Awate, a native of Tessenei, a member of a Bani Amir clan, and an activist since the mid-1950s, launched the first open battle against the Ethiopian army. The episode was later adopted as the starting point of the Eritrean struggle for independence.[1]

The exiles were soon active in getting organized politically, and by late 1963 the recognized bodies of the Eritrean movement had been established. Chief of these was the ten-member Supreme Council (*al-Majlis al-a'la*), based in Khartoum, of the ELF. The Supreme Council was made up of five secretariats: military affairs, intelligence, information, finance, and foreign relations.[2] Idris Muhammad Adam (b. 1918)—a member of the Bani Amir tribe, former president (1955–1956) of the defunct Eritrean assembly, an active leader throughout the 1950s and 1960s, and an exile in Cairo before the annexation—was chosen as its president.

The members of the Supreme Council included several prominent personages. The Protestant Walda-Ab Walda-Mariam, a onetime LPP leader and former president of the Eritrean Trade Union Confederation who had also left for Cairo in the late 1950s, was appointed head of the Foreign Mission. A prominent Muslim member was Uthman Salih Sabi, a member of the Assawurta tribe and former ML leader. Uthman was appointed secretary general and roving ambassador. Neither Walda-Ab (based in Cairo) nor Uthman (based in Beirut) was particularly close to Idris Adam, and neither took much part in the deliberations of the Supreme Council, which was dominated by members of the Bani Amir tribe. Idris Uthman Qladyus, another Muslim and an associate of Idris Adam, was made secretary and adviser on military affairs.

The Supreme Council maintained indirect control over the fighters in the field by providing the movement with political legitimacy, finances, supplies, and arms, as well as through occasional involvement in tactical planning. Furthermore, since it designated the fighters who were to undergo advanced training in Arab (and sometimes communist) countries, the exiles had a hand in shaping the new generation of field commanders who would gradually replace the old and rather parochial tribal military leaders.[3]

Another process in the mid-1960s that contributed significantly to the emerging Eritrean movement was the growing tendency of young Eritrean Christians to identify with the cause of separatism. This trend should be seen in the context of Haile Selassie's shortcomings as a source of identification for modern, educated youngsters. In Addis Ababa his regime was strong and efficient enough to quell the activities of resentful students and recruit them on graduation. In the cities of Eritrea, however, the attempt to impose medieval emperorship was opposed by proud young members of an intelligentsia that had lived for seven decades under European administration and had, for more than two decades, been accustomed to quite a high standard of political life. Many young members of the urban Christian communities now regretted their fathers' zeal for reunification. Realizing that Eritrea was an ex-colony in a continent where almost all ex-colonies were now independent states, they flocked to join the ranks of the ELF.[4]

The growth of the ELF, from an estimated nine hundred fighters in 1961–1962 to some two thousand in 1967 brought with it an increase in internal diversity.[5] As yet, the groups of different tribal, religious, regional, linguistic, cultural, and social backgrounds who resisted the Ethiopian authorities and army were barely united by the still vague concept of Eritrean nationalism. In 1965, in order to minimize the risk of internal disputes, the Supreme Council established five military regions (*mintaka askariyya* or *willaya*). Region I appears to have comprised the territories adjacent to the Sudanese border; region II the territories in and around the town of Keren; region III the northern Sahil; region IV the Massawa coast and the Danakil Desert; and region V, centered on Asmara, the Christian-populated highlands.[6] The Supreme Council controlled the military regions through an intermediate body named the Revolutionary Command, based in the Sudanese frontier town of Kassala. Among the members of both bodies in the mid-1960s were such leaders as Taha Muhammad Nur, Muhammad Salih Hamid, Sayyid Muhammad, Abd al-Karim Muhammad, Muhammad Kiyar, Umar Hamid Azaz, Omaro Alionaro, and Waldai Kassai.[7] A training and enlisting committee was also established under Umar Muhammad Ali Damir, to encourage cooperation between the regions.[8] Each region was led by a military commander (the Christian Waldai Kassai over region V and the Muslim Umar Hamid Azaz over region II; the names of the commanders of the other regions are not known), aided by a political commissioner. This decentralized structure proved quite successful in coping with the challenge of growth and diversity as long as military action was confined to sporadic hit-and-run operations in the countryside and as long as the old generation of military commanders controlled units in the field.

By 1967, this was no longer the case. In the period following the Six Day War, events in the Middle East began to affect Eritrean affairs increasingly, and this was reflected in an intensification of combat activities by both the ELF and the Ethiopian army. The closing of the Suez Canal was economically disastrous for Eritrea, and the widespread unemployment that came in its wake caused a surge in popular support for the rebels.[9] However, this unprecedented swelling of the rebels' ranks coupled with the emergence of a new generation of Eritrean field commanders exposed the loose organizational structure of the ELF to strong internal pressures. Thus began a period characterized by splits along the lines of ethnic, religious, and regional differences, conflicts fired by personal rivalries for power and control over the movement, and a growing generation gap between the young military leaders in the field and the veteran politicians and fund raisers abroad.

The first signs that the Christians were experiencing difficulties in the movement appeared early in 1967. The main supporter and supplier of the movement at that time was Syria's Pan-Arabist Ba'thist regime, and Eritrean youngsters were trained at the Syrian military academy in Aleppo. Since Ba'thist doctrine regarded Eritrea as an integral part of the Arab world, the training in Syria was conducted in Arabic, and in accordance with the instructions of Idris Qladyus, the military secretary of the Revolutionary Command, only Muslim fighters were sent to be trained there. The Christians were trained in Eritrean camps in the Sudan. There they found that the use of Tigrinya was forbidden, and they were told that the aim of the ELF was to Arabize Eritrea.[10] In June 1967, when Ethiopian authorities proclaimed an amnesty, some one hundred Christian fighters (and a few Muslims) deserted the ELF and surrendered, including the Christian commander of region V, Waldai Kassai, who was a member of the Revolutionary Command.[11]

The Ethiopian government—for reasons to be dealt with below—failed to comprehend reality in the province and was therefore unable to exploit the growing split in the Eritrean movement. Instead, the backward image of Haile Selassie's regime and its policy of Amharization alienated the young genera- tion of Christians; in the mid-1970s, following the revolution in Ethiopia, they would join the Eritrean nationalist cause en masse. In the meantime, however, active Christian participation in the ELF was limited primarily to the regions of Asmara, the Sahil, and Keren.

By 1968, the rifts had widened sufficiently to require structural change in the ELF. Particularly, the gap between the emerging generation of young field commanders and leaders in exile had increased.[12] The latter were accused of encouraging "sophisticated divisiveness" (as reflected in the system of regions) in order to advance their own personal interests and to distribute the move- ment's money and other privileges (such as military training courses abroad) among their associates.[13] Resentment against the Supreme Council and the Revolutionary Command was especially strong in the eastern regions. The Bani Amir Muslims of the west were strongly represented on the Supreme Council by Idris Adam and Idris Qladyus and thus had less cause for discon- tent. Furthermore, it was widely rumored in the east that the policy of allocating more resources for the anti-Ethiopian struggle in the west was ultimately aimed at political compromise with the Ethiopians at the expense of the nationalist aspirations of the coastal population and the highlanders.[14] Thus, in early September 1968, discontented representatives of regions III, IV, and V convened in the Ansaba area; the western Bani Amir–populated regions I and II refused to attend.[15] (In fact, violent clashes had occurred during 1967 between fighters of the eastern and western regions.[16])

The Ansaba meeting called for abolition of the regions and proclaimed the Tripartite Union (*al-Itbibad al-muthallath*). However, the regional commands were not completely abolished. Members of the Tripartite Union who were natives of the Baraka region and the areas around Keren (previously part of regions II and III) remained in separate camps under their leader, Adam Salih. (They were later to be known as Obelyun after a place in their country.) Natives of the coastal lowlands of region IV, the Massawiyun ("people of Massawa"), remained under the command of Muhammad Umar Abdallah. Fighters from the central highlands (region V) were led by Ibrahim Tewald and Isayas Afawarq.[17] Although the leaders of the new union were sworn rivals, they were well aware that disunity reduced the effectiveness of the movement and that in consequence they could probably recruit and train only one-third of the able-bodied sympathizers. They therefore called for the organization of a national congress to be attended by all groups and sectors, Christian and Muslim, and aimed at achieving fundamental democratization and a transfer of political leadership from the exiles to the field commanders.

The establishment of the Tripartite Union was in open defiance of the Supreme Council, and the new group sent three young fighters—Isayas Afawarq (a Christian from region V who was later to become a key figure in Eritrean history) and the Muslims Muhammad Umar Abdallah (region V) and Ali Amru—to Khartoum to establish contact with sympathetic members of the Supreme Council.[18] These included the Cairo-based Christian Walda-Ab Walda-Mariam (who together with Muhammad Said Nawud and Muhammad Salih Mahmud was in opposition to Idris Adam); the Muslim leader Uthman Salih Sabi; and the Christian Tedla Bairu, a former UP leader and later the first chief executive in Eritrea under the federation, who had joined the rebels in 1967.

From then on, political developments within the Eritrean movement intensified. Responding to the challenge, the other members of the Supreme Council, Idris Adam, Idris Qladyus, Sayyid Muhammad, Uthman Ali Ahmad, Salih Ayay, Muhammad Salih Hamid, and Mahmud Ismail (till then said to be temporizing about convening a national conference[19]), started preparations to hold a conference in a region under the control of their Bani Amir supporters.

Walda-Ab Walda-Mariam, now allied with the Tripartite Union, denounced this step strongly. In an open letter dated 8 March 1969 addressed to Idris Adam and his associates, he accused them of selfishly pursuing power by, among other things, encouraging nepotism and ignoring the views and interests of the new generation of field commanders. Three of the five regions and Eritrean students abroad had rejected their leadership—the latter at a preliminary conference of the Eritrean Students' General Union, held in Damascus in December 1968 (most probably under the auspices of Walda-Ab himself).[20] In the name of both the Tripartite and the Students' Union, Walda-Ab demanded the formation of a new preparatory committee and the abolition of the regions as a condition for his participation in the national congress. He called on the Supreme Command to permit units in the field to send two delegates for every 100 fighters and students abroad to send ten delegates (five from the Middle East and five from Europe).

Idris Adam rejected Walda-Ab's demands, but the influence of the Supreme Council was waning. Even the young fighters of the western regions were no longer ready to accept its leadership, and the pressure of field commanders made the convening of a national conference on Eritrean soil inevitable.

On 25 August 1969, the First National Congress of the ELF opened in the Adobha plain near Agordat (a Bani Amir–controlled area). The delegates included representatives of the Tripartite Union, but this first popular meeting of the various Eritrean groups was fated to become a major landmark in divisiveness. The outcome of the Adobha congress was an open schism between the men in the field and the exiles and an even worse division between west and east.

During the discussions, fighters from throughout the province denounced the Supreme Council and the Revolutionary Command, accusing them of impotence and of fomenting rivalries. Both were officially abolished, as were the five regions. The Supreme Council and the Revolutionary Command were replaced by a new, 38-member General Command (al-Qiyyada al-'ama), consisting exclusively of field commanders. The congress decided that a unified Eritrean Liberation Army would be established, with supratribal and supraethnic brigade-size units and auxiliary units. An ex-student at Cairo University, Muhammad Ahmad Abduh, was appointed commander in chief of the unified army for a period of one year.[21] The triumph of the fighters over the exiles was illustrated by a resolution proclaiming the General Command's intention to assume control of the movement's foreign offices.

Yet, despite the fighters' proclaimed unity, the congress was marred by intrigue and suspicion and resulted in the ascendancy of regions I and II over the much smaller group of delegates representing the Tripartite Union. Of the 38 men elected to the General Command, no fewer than 20 were from the two western regions. Prominent among them were Ahmad Muhammad Ibrahim (chairman of the General Command), Mahmud Ibrahim (head of the Political Bureau), Muhammad Abduh, Salih Ibrahim, Muhammad Burhan Abd al-Rahman, the Christian Tesfai Tekla, Abd al-Qadir Ramadan, and Said Salih.[22]

A few weeks after the end of the congress, open hostilities emerged. A major reason for the lack of trust was the persistent rumor, which spread throughout the province, that the leaders of the western regions were in constant touch with Idris Adam and were negotiating a deal with the Ethiopians in which the ELF would stop disturbing communications with the ports of Assab and Massawa in exchange for a free hand in the west.[23] Muhammad Abduh was accused of negotiating to this effect with the U.S. consul in Asmara, Murray Jackson. The chief advisers of Eritrea's Ethiopian governor, *Ras* Asrate Kassa—namely, Tesfa-Yohannes Berhe, Hamid Faraj, and Muhammad Umar Qadi—were said to be in contact with members of the General Command.[24] In fact, as discussed below, sometime in early 1970, the Ethiopian *ras* traveled clandestinely to a remote town near the Sudanese border to discuss the matter with Idris Adam.

As a result of these developments, tension prevailed in the new General Command. By late 1969, six of the eighteen leaders of the Tripartite Union had been arrested, two others had been killed by partisans from the western regions, and the rest had fled. Two of the latter, Isayas Afawarq and Abbera Makonnen, surreptitiously returned to the Asmara region, but other fighters from eastern Eritrea in attendance at Adobha managed to return to their regions only in the middle of 1970.[25]

The Adobha conference and its consequences were a blow not only for Walda-Ab but also for Uthman Salih Sabi, the relentlessly energetic secretary general and roving ambassador of the movement. Uthman, who was related to the Assawurta tribe of the Massawa coastal area, refused to accept the line adopted by the new General Command.[26] Although he continued to portray himself as a spokesman for the whole movement and a persistent advocate of Eritrean unity, after the Adobha congress Uthman started working for the coastal Muslims and Christian highlanders, both of whom had been defeated at Adobha.

Uthman had already established himself in Arab capitals as the most prominent Eritrean in exile. His position was based on his competence as a fund raiser and on his repeatedly declared belief that the Eritreans were Arabs and their war was an integral part of the Middle Eastern struggle to fulfill Arab nationalism.[27] Uthman Sabi's self-identification as an Arab stemmed from his origins in the coastal region, where Islam had taken hold in the seventh century and Arabic was widely spoken. He himself was born some seven miles from Massawa in the town of Harkiku,[28] for centuries the symbol of Eritrea's affiliation with the Middle Eastern Muslim world. His native language was Arabic, and he had a Syrian wife. (The Bani Amir of western Eritrea, in contrast, had no Arab affiliations and were converted to Islam only in the 1820s.)

Uthman's insistence that the Eritreans were Arabs and that their struggle against the Ethiopia of Haile Selassie was part of the war on Zionism made him a welcome guest in Arab capitals and in the camps of the Palestine Liberation Organization (PLO). It was, in fact, in a PLO camp in Amman that he laid the foundation of a new Eritrean organization, the future EPLF. Aided by veteran Christian leader Tedla Bairu, as well as by Taha Muhammad Nur and Uthman Idris Khiyar, Uthman Sabi convened what he called the First Conference of the Eritrean Liberation Front Political Offices (15–18 November 1969).[29] (He referred to the Adobha congress as "a military meeting."[30]) Declaring themselves the new political leadership of the Eritrean movement, the participants formed the General Secretariat of the Eritrean Liberation Front.

It was, however, quite obvious that they did not represent the whole move-ment, but were a regrouping of the opposition to the General Command. From 2 to 24 June 1970, when the majority of the fighters of the Tripartite Union were finally back in their regions, representatives of the Massawiyun and of Uthman Sabi's General Secretariat met at Sadouha Aila, south of Massawa, and established a new movement, the Popular Liberation Forces (PLF), with Uthman at the head of its Foreign Mission.[31]

The establishment of the PLF made it virtually impossible to reach a territorial compromise between the Eritrean separatists and Addis Ababa. Since the PLF soon began to attract young Christian Eritreans from urban centers, its formation led both to the strengthening of the Eritrean movement and to an immediate escalation in the war.

The establishment of the PLF in a PLO base symbolized the growing relations between the two movements. Uthman Sabi spared no effort in promoting this cooperation. He even sent PLF fighters to help the PLO in Jordan during the September 1970 clash with the Jordanian army.[32] These relations were, however, far more significant militarily and otherwise in Eritrea. Due to PLO training and advice (and also due to the provision of arms and finances by Libya, the Sudan, South Yemen, and others—support that had intensified in 1969 for reasons discussed below), the establishment of the PLF marked an important turning point. Until then, for instance, Eritrean fighters had rarely used mines and explosives, confining themselves instead to shooting at passing vehicles from a distance. This was no longer the case after 1969; by that time the number of Eritreans who had received training abroad in advanced guerrilla tactics had increased considerably. (Arab assistance in this area was less effective than that rendered by the Cubans and the Chinese; both countries invited sizable numbers of carefully selected Eritrean young-sters for comprehensive guerrilla training in the late 1960s.)

The chance to travel abroad attracted many young members of the Eritrean intelligentsia. Together with financial and military aid, such foreign support—radical Arab or communist—was a major factor in developing the Eritrean organizations and movement. With their new methods and weapons, the Eritreans began executing spectacular acts of sabotage and terrorism, including hijacking of planes, kidnapping of foreign diplomats, blowing up of bridges in front of cameras, and ambushing and assassinating Ethiopian functionaries and collaborators.[33]

The growing split within the Eritrean movement was a crucial factor in the increase in the number of actions, as rival factions competed for popular support. Much to the tragedy of Eritrea, the increased violence played into the hands of hard-liners in the Ethiopian camp; in Addis Ababa, as in the camps of Eritrean nationalists, the hard-liners seeking a military solution would prevail.

One of the most spectacular terrorist acts of the time was performed by a young schoolteacher, Isayas Afawarq (b. 1946), an important leader of the now defunct Tripartite Union. As a youngster, Isayas had been influenced by a Marxist-oriented economist from Asmara, Dr. Biasolo, a half-caste business-man and a disillusioned ex-member of the UP.[34] On 14 April 1970, in a bar in downtown Asmara, Isayas machine-gunned two ex-judges who had sentenced some ELF guerrillas to death. (According to one version, the murder was committed by Isayas's associates.[35]) Isayas fled Asmara, and in the districts of Hamasen and Sarai, together with some eight young commanders (notably his associates Ibrahim Tewald and Irmayas Debbasi), he managed to organize a group of a few hundred Christian warriors.[36]

Throughout 1970 and 1971, Isayas and his associates were active in the Eritrean highlands and around Keren, successfully fighting the Ethiopian army and terrorizing the population. In November 1970, a unit belonging to these forces, reputedly led by Irmayas Debbasi, ambushed and killed the commander of the Ethiopian army in the province,[37] an event that greatly helped the cause of hard-liners in Addis Ababa.

In early March 1971, at a meeting in Obel attended by hundreds of fighters from the Baraka region and the central highlands, Isayas and his associates managed to outvote Muhammad Abduh and two other members of the General Command, who tried to win the meeting's support for their Eritrean Liberation Army,[38] and proclaimed the establishment of the Eritrean Liberation Forces–Obel. Isayas himself, however, was not influential enough in Baraka to obtain full control over the Obelyun. The following July he established his own group, Nehnan Elamann, consisting of Christian highlanders.[39]

At the Obel meeting, the General Command had lost control over many of the fighters in region II (Keren), who now started cooperating with Isayas. It was, however, somewhat more successful in undermining Uthman Sabi's influence in Arab capitals. The General Command sent missions to open offices in Cairo and Algeria, but their most significant achievement was in winning the sympathy of the Ba'thist regimes in Syria and Iraq.[40] This was due partly to the hard work of Salih Ayay in Damascus and Mahmud Ismail in Baghdad (the heads of the respective offices), but primarily to the fact that almost all Eritrean graduates of the Syrian and Iraqi military academies were associated with the General Command. However, in Beirut, with the PLO, in Libya, in Saudi Arabia (thanks to close personal ties with King Faisal), and in South Yemen, Uthman Sabi continued to have more influence than the General Command.[41] In this diplomatic warfare, the youngsters of the General Command joined hands with Idris Adam and his associates from the defunct Supreme Council.

On the home front, despite Muhammad Abduh's failure to build the Eritrean Liberation Army,[42] the General Command was determined to impose unity. Members of the General Command met twice with Isayas in early 1971 in an attempt to organize the first Eritrean National Congress, a task with which they had been charged by the Adobha conference.[43] They finally managed to organize a preparatory conference (27 May–4 June 1971), which was attended by representatives of Isayas's Eritrean Liberation Forces–Obel.[44] By that time, however, Isayas and his men had developed contacts with Uthman Sabi, mainly through Isayas's friend, Asmarom Amara.[45] Uthman, using Libyan money and South Yemeni camps and ports, proved far more useful to Isayas in arming and training his guerrillas than did the General Command and its supporters. It was, therefore, quite natural that by September 1971 Isayas and the General Command were in open conflict.[46] When the General Command convened what it called the First National Congress of the ELF at Ar near the Sudanese border (14 October–12 November 1971), Isayas and his associates were absent.

The 561 delegates at the First National Congress reputedly represented such sectors as soldiers, village committees, women's groups, and the like. The congress was reportedly conducted in a democratic spirit, with free and lengthy debate. Practically, however, the significance of the occasion lay in its determination of the organizational structure of one of the two major Eritrean organizations, the ELF-RC, which has existed since then.

The congress resolved to abolish the General Command and form a Revolutionary Council (RC) chaired by the veteran Idris Adam (who back in late 1969 had been among those members of the defunct Supreme Council who recognized the Adobha resolutions.[47] His young associate, the Christian Heruy Tedla, was made his deputy and head of the Political Bureau. Abdallah Idris was appointed head of the Military Bureau. (Among other members of the council were Ahmad Nasir, Salih Ayay, Umar Ali, Tesfai Tekla, Abd al-Qadir Ramadan, Muhammad Salih Hamid, and Ja'far Muhammad Nur.)

The creators of the ELF-RC conceived the organization as the only true representative of Eritrean nationalism and resolved that "the Eritrean arena can tolerate only one revolution led by one organization with a single command." Denouncing Uthman's PLF and Isayas's followers, the delegates further resolved that "the Command stemming from the Congress shall have full powers to take military measures to ensure the unity of the organization and the unity of the revolution."[48] Muhammad Abduh and his units were charged with pursuing and destroying those Eritreans who refused to join the ELF-RC.

Following the establishment of the ELF-RC, the forces of the Obelyun and of Isayas Afawarq united with the PLF. At a seven-day meeting that opened on 21 December 1971 between the Eritrean Liberation Forces–Obel and Isayas's men, the latter strongly denounced the "false conference" of the ELF-RC, especially the tendency of the RC "to push us towards a military settlement for the problems of the revolution . . . and the bodily liquidation of the national movement."[49] Isayas's associate and former superior in the Tripartite Union, Ibrahim Tewald, a firm advocate of compromise with the ELF-RC, was found poisoned.[50] In a series of meetings with representatives of the PLF from 3 to 12 February 1972, these two organizations merged to form the Eritrean People's Liberation Forces (EPLF).[51] It was decided that the Foreign Mission, which would represent the Eritrean revolution abroad, would be under the presidency of Walda-Ab Walda-Mariam with Uthman Salih Sabi as secretary general and official spokesman of the revolution. Other members of the Foreign Mission included Muhammad Said Nawud and Muhammad Said Idris in Beirut, Umar Muhammad al-Bari in Libya, and Taha Muhammad Nur in Cairo. The field forces of the various groups in the EPLF were said to be united under the command of a military committee headed by Isayas, whose members reputedly included Ramadan Muhammad Nur, Mesfin Iyoas, Ali Berhan, and Adam Salih. In practice, however, the Obelyun, the Massawiyun and the Tigrean highlanders remained organized in different, even rival units.[52] According to an EPLF publication, only in early 1972 (possibly within the framework of the early February meetings with Uthman's men) did fighters of these three groups meet for the first time and agree to form a "united front." Two of the three merged in 1973, and the third group eventually joined them a year later.[53]

The establishment of the ELF-RC and later the EPLF did not end the period of organizational fluidity in the Eritrean movement. The two organizations were merely amalgams of different groups and were far from internally stable; moreover, the rivalry and enmity between them grew constantly. Efforts to ease the tension or reach some understanding (such as the negotiations conducted between Tesfai Tekla and Abd al-Qadir Ramadan of the ELF-RC and Mesfin Iyoas of the EPLF in February 1973 or another effort made the following July) proved futile.

The gap between the organizations, as well as the endless internal rivalries,[54] arose from the pluralist nature of Eritrea, with each faction having its own interests. In essence, the ELF-RC seemed to be a western Eritrean organization combining young, local fighters with the older members of the Supreme Council. The EPLF was a marriage of convenience among Christian highlanders, coastal Muslims, and another faction of exiles. The situation was made even more complex by the network of personal rivalries and religious, ethnic, and other differences.

Ideological differences between the two organizations also emerged during this period. The EPLF had to make extensive use of Marxist phraseology to explain how more than half of its fighters were Christian Tigreans while its

Foreign Mission was dominated by an Arab nationalist. The ELF-RC, consisting predominantly of Bani Amir fighters, was closer than the EPLF to the Pan-Arabist regimes of Syria and Iraq but was less committed to Arabism (and to Marxism). The ELF-RC emphasized Eritrean uniqueness and urged Eritrean unity (under its exclusive hegemony), while the EPLF saw the Eritrean struggle more in the context of an all–Middle Eastern social and nationalist revolution and believed revolutionary changes in Eritrean society essential to national or organizational unity. These ideological differences would become even more important factors after the 1974 revolution in Ethiopia.

It was for these reasons that between 1972 and 1974 the Eritrean nationalists were busier fighting each other than resisting the Ethiopian authorities. As soon as the EPLF was established in February 1972, the ELF-RC instigated an open and active war in an effort to enforce unity.[55] Clashes between units and acts of assassination on both sides, as well as bloody internal battles and purges,[56] were to continue until October 1974, when a major battle between the two organizations and other developments related to the revolution in Ethiopia would conclude the fratricidal fighting in Eritrea. The hostilities claimed the lives of hundreds of Eritrean fighters (according to one estimate, there were as many as three thousand casualties[57]), and virtually destroyed the military ability of the Eritrean nationalists. Indeed, in March 1974, an important Eritrean leader admitted that the chances of fulfilling secessionist goals were slight. He thought that if the Ethiopian government of Haile Selassie had adopted a flexible and a more democratic approach to the Eritrean question, the Eritreans would have abandoned the battle for secession or even autonomy.[58]

The number of Eritrean separatists in this period is hard to estimate. According to their own sources, however, and to sympathizers, it never exceeded two thousand. Many of these were in any case merely following a long tradition of *shifta* (banditry) rather than pursuing the fulfillment of modern nationalism. Even in their finest hour, they were no threat to the Ethiopian hold over the province.

The main participants in the story of Eritreanism in the 1960s, the leaders in exile, had marginal influence on the Eritrean populace, who by and large learned to live with the sporadic terrorism exercised by local activists. The diminishing significance of the exiles was to be exposed in the second half of the 1970s, when the strengthening of the nationalist movement in the field would increasingly reduce their influence.

Eritrean nationalism during the 1960s was too weak to be of strategic importance, but the vitality and persistence of the small groups of separatists, combined with foreign support from radical Arab and communist countries, was sufficient to make its influence felt. Chapter Five discusses the role of the radical Arabs in detail; here it is sufficient to note that in the opinion of many

Western experts, it was the Soviets, and up to 1971 the Chinese, who stood behind this activity.[59] However, it was not enough to change the situation in the Horn of Africa.

At this stage, when the nationalist movements were still girding their loins, so to speak, the Ethiopian government could have controlled the situation if it had adopted a more sophisticated and flexible policy. Instead, its brutal efforts to quell the separatists served only to fan the flame of Eritrean nationalism. Moreover, in Eritrea as in Ethiopia, rivalries and intrigues created splits and conflicts in which the hard-liners prevailed—the inevitable response of the ascendancy of hard-liners in the opposite camp.

3. Addis Ababa and Eritrea, 1962–1973

The Eritrean separatist movement constituted a triple threat to Haile Selassie's regime. First, it threatened Ethiopia's military and economic security. Eritrea contained Ethiopia's only ports and in economic importance was second only to the metropolitan province of Shoa.

Second, to Addis Ababa, any compromise based on recognition of the Eritrean right to self-determination had disastrous implications for the very existence of the empire. The Ethiopian kingdom that emerged in the late nineteenth century was a melange of diverse ethnic, religious, linguistic, and social groupings. Consequently, the Ethiopian government of Haile Selassie had to abandon the centuries-old concept of Ethiopian-Christian self-identification and adopt, as was later to take place all over Africa, the concept of territorial nationalism—at least in theory. According to the first article of the 1931 constitution, "The territory of Ethiopia, in its entirety, is, from one end to the other, subject to the Government of his Majesty the Emperor. All the natives of Ethiopia, subjects of the empire, form together the Ethiopian Nation."[1] Yielding to the Eritrean demand to be recognized as a different nation could well encourage separatism among such groups as Somalis, Tigreans, Oromos, and others. In 1967, for this reason, the Ethiopian parliament rejected the idea of granting even limited powers of self-administration to the various districts on the grounds that "while it is clear that Ethiopia has existed for the last 3,000 years . . . it is also known that Ethiopia is comprised of different tribal groups which were far from regarding one another as members of the same nation, viewing each other as outsiders, having different outlooks and with no free intermingling: and to create separate and autonomous *awrajas* [districts] before the people know one another . . . would be encouraging separatist tendencies."² Only in 1976 almost two years after the deposition of Haile Selassie, would the new military and revolutionary government adopt limited self-administration in order to ease separatist tensions—but this action came too late to affect the Eritrean situation.

Third, the Eritrean struggle constituted a serious threat to the Ethiopian regime's concept of absolutist emperorship. Throughout the 1950s and 1960s, Haile Selassie did very little to compensate the Eritreans for their loss of internal political freedom. He was well aware that the separatist organizations presented not only a different concept of nationalism, but also a different ideology. Ideas of revolution, occasionally couched in Marxist phraseology, had implications for not only any future regime in an independent Eritrea but also the future of the entire region. Because Eritrean nationalists conceived their struggle in the context of a revolution embracing the whole area, opposition groups in Ethiopia, such as students, tended to sympathize with the Eritrean cause.

Because of these threats, the consensus prevailing within Haile Selassie's political establishment was that there was no room for compromise with the Eritrean organizations on the issue of self-determination. Since the Eritrean nationalists were also uncompromising, the continuation of war was inevitable.

Essentially, Ethiopia's policy on the Eritrean problem was to ignore it. Government spokesmen and the media simply avoided the matter and, whenever it was raised by others, dismissed the Eritrean nationalists as *shifta* (highwaymen or outlaws) or presented them as bloodthirsty and greedy robbers in the service of Ethiopia's external enemies.

Unfortunately for Ethiopia, ignoring the problem did nothing to solve it. It seems, however, that this policy sprang not so much from tactical considerations as from the basic practical approach of the imperial authorities. According to a well-informed source, Haile Selassie's government never discussed the Eritrean problem in the entire period under review and had no comprehensive plan for dealing with it. Any Ethiopian action in Eritrea was not part of a series of planned steps, but rather the outcome of a continuous and fluctuating struggle for power and influence among those involved.

Militarily, too, the policy was to ignore the facts. Throughout the entire period, the Ethiopian army made less than a token effort to collect information on the *shifta* and their organizations. Military commanders knew very little about what and whom they were facing. The army was therefore able only to react to initiatives taken by the rebels. There was no long-range planning and no coordination between the various branches.

The main reason for this lack of planning and consistency stemmed from the structure of the Ethiopian political and military establishments. Many observers have dealt with the subject of intrigues, jealousies, and rivalries as a shaping force in Ethiopian politics. Such rivalries and intrigues, which served to inhibit creative initiative, intensified in the last decade of Haile Selassie's rule. The main issue was the competition for positions that could serve as springboards to power following the death of the aging absolutist. However, the emperor—who for obvious reasons encouraged this competition—refused to abdicate even when over eighty, and the tangled web of intrigues entrapped and paralyzed the jockeying rivals, ultimately causing the demise of Haile Selassie's political establishment. Throughout the period, it was these rivalries that determined the government's approach to the Eritrean problem.

One of the most important rivalries was between the members of the so-called Shoan nobility group, which consisted of some of the emperor's relatives and members of the old leading families, and the members of a loosely knit group of leading politicians and generals, some of whom the emperor had promoted from obscurity. The most prominent and active member of the Shoan nobility group was *Ras* Asrate Kassa. Other important personalities belonging to this group were Lt. Gen. Abiy Ababa, *Lij* Endalkatchaw Makonnen, Maj. Gen. Assefa Demise, and Lt. Gen. Dabbab Haila-Mariam. The rival group, headed by Prime Minister (since 1961) *Tsahafe Te'zaz* Aklilu Habta-Wald, included almost all important ministers in Aklilu's government, such as his brother Akala-Warq Habta-Wald, Foreign Minister Katama Yifru, and Minister of Commerce and Industry Yilma Deresa, as well as some prominent army generals, such as Lt. Gen. Assefa Ayene, who was chief of staff in the late 1960s.

Neither group was cohesive, and each lacked internal trust and cooperation. Since the political order after Haile Selassie's death was a matter of speculation, no one was ready to commit himself fully, and no one was openly recognized as a leader (as the Amharic saying goes: "When hyenas hunt, they march side by side"). However, it was widely assumed that Asrate and Aklilu were the leaders of these groups, and that they would contend for the position of kingmaker and power behind the throne following the emperor's death. The intense rivalry that developed between Asrate and Aklilu did much to mold Ethiopia's policy in Eritrea.

In 1964, Asrate (then still only a *dadjazmach*) was appointed crown representative (*enderase*) and governor-general in Eritrea, a position that he held until late 1970. Asrate was considered the living embodiment of loyalty to Haile Selassie. His father, *Ras* Kassa Hailu, had had a stronger claim to the throne than Haile Selassie did, but had done more than anyone else to ensure that Haile Selassie would come to power. In the postwar period, Asrate succeeded his father as one of the emperor's most trusted officials and advisers. Since 1942 he had held a succession of major posts in the provinces and the Senate;

and it was he who had masterminded the action against the 1960 rebels, thus helping to save Haile Selassie's crown.[3] In Eritrea, Asrate Kassa immediately started working toward his dual aims: quelling the separatists and turning Eritrea into a solid power base for himself.

Asrate's declared long-range objective was to see his personal friend and Haile Selassie's only surviving son, Crown Prince *Maridazmach* Asfa-Wassan, as the next emperor, with himself as the future strongman. (It was widely and persistently speculated that he was aiming even higher.) In the meantime, however, his power in Addis Ababa was diminishing, and Prime Minister Aklilu Habta-Wald, who had other ideas regarding future candidates for the emperorship, was gaining ascendance in the capital. In 1966 the emperor gave Aklilu the right to appoint ministers. In the same year, however, he promoted Asrate to *ras*. In order to advance his cause, Asrate started modernizing and centralizing the government of Eritrea, with the aim of creating his own principality there with local military forces answerable to him. Mixing an enlightened approach to the needs of the various Eritrean communities with an aura of paternalism, he played the role of benevolent king with all due pomp and circumstance.

In the sphere of administration, Asrate appointed local Eritreans to the position of director general of each of the province's eight districts (*awrajas*): Hamasen, Sarai, Akalla-Guzai, Keren, Agordat, Sahil, Massawa, and Assab.[4] Eritreans (preferably Christian Tigreans) were also appointed to other important functions—notably, *Dadjazmach* Tesfa-Yohannes Berhe as Asrate's deputy and *Dadjazmach* Haragot Abbay as mayor of Asmara.[5] These functionaries and other advisers from the province formed a local "cabinet" chaired by Asrate. Despite his policy of favoring Eritreans in administrative positions, Asrate was clearly reluctant to soften the policy of Amharizing education and culture; the official use and teaching of Tigrinya, Tigre, and Arabic was forbidden.[6]

In the sphere of economics, Asrate did his best to strengthen Eritrea's financial independence from Addis Ababa. On his initiative, the province now had its own budget, based on the fiscal policy set forth by his cabinet. His efforts to maintain financial independence occasionally included a refusal to transfer the revenues of the Eritrean ports of Massawa and Assab to the capital. This so angered the prime minister that the emperor himself was forced to intervene.

Asrate's main problem was that regular army forces in Eritrea answered to Aklilu's government. The regular units stationed in Eritrea belonged to the 2d Division (one of four army divisions), which was charged with defending the country's northern frontier and maintaining internal security in the northern regions. Until the deterioration of events in Eritrea in 1969, two of the division's three brigades were stationed in Tigre and Bagemdir. Since the mid-1960s the 2d Division had been commanded by Maj. Gen. Ergetu Tshome, an Amharan of humble origin, with Brig. Gen. Marid Gizaw as second in command. The divisional headquarters was in Asmara, and up to 1969 the Eritrean brigade's three battalions were stationed in Asmara, Keren, and on the Massawa-Asmara road. The rest of the area was covered by occasional patrols and company-size stations in places such as Agordat and Tessenei. In 1967 the Tigrean brigade was moved to Agordat, and most of the Bagemdir brigade were also transferred to Eritrea.

Thus, the most important of Asrate's efforts to secure his own position in Eritrea was the building of well-trained armed units directly loyal to him. In late 1965, following an intensification of rebel activities, he formed a special counterinsurgency force, known as the "commandos" or "101" and funded by an allocation from the Eritrean budget. By the end of the 1960s, it was a battalion-size unit comprising nine superbly trained companies. Its central base was in Decamere, where the recruits—mostly Christian Eritreans—were trained by Israeli experts. They wore uniforms different from the regular army's and used different weaponry. Officially, the commandos were affiliated with the Eritrean police, an exclusively Eritrean force in charge of daily security in urban centers.[7] The formation and building of the commandos— also known as the "governor's private army"—were a major achievement.

Another Ethiopian group under Asrate's control that dealt with the Eritrean separatists was the General Security Service, which was established in Eritrea on his initiative and funded locally. Throughout this period, the service was headed by Amda-Mikael Belhachaw, a man totally loyal to Asrate. The organization was in charge of counterinsurgency activities and had its own intelligence service based on spies in various urban and rural centers in Eritrea. The Ethiopian air force (based in Asmara) and navy (based in Massawa) each answered to its own headquarters. The various bodies involved in the war against the Eritrean separatists became immersed in Ethiopia's complex network of rivalries, and Asrate's persistent efforts to achieve coordination among them and to establish a joint command were systematically opposed by his rivals. Although he ultimately succeeded in 1967, the coordinating body he established was virtually ignored and occasionally even misinformed by many of the commanders concerned.

This situation was not due to any lack of administrative ability, but reflected Ethiopian politics in general. The old Ethiopian system of *shum shir* (appoint and transfer) reached rare perfection under Haile Selassie, whose aim was to neutralize the members of the establishment by fomenting mutual distrust. With this objective in mind, the emperor made sure to visit Eritrea twice a year, taking advantage of the opportunity to make appointments and changes without notifying the *ras*. Every prominent functionary reported separately; the very idea of a coordinating body ran counter to the political system.

This carefully planned lack of coordination was not the only reason for the Ethiopian failure to cope with the separatist movement. Another major factor was the structure of the Ethiopian army. On paper, the army consisted of divisions, brigades, and battalions. In practice, and especially in Eritrea, the combat army was made up of companies. Battalion-level commanders were considered to have risen so high in society as to be above the business of waging war; officers from the rank of lieutenant colonel up enjoyed very high salaries and gifts of land and had very little incentive to advance the professional ability of their subordinates or to lead them in battle. Many of them found ways to gain financial advantage by monopolizing their units' supplies of food and equipment and accumulated wealth at the expense of the rank and file. It was the company commanders who led patrols and other operations. Usually in Eritrea a company would leave camp for a month-long routine counterinsurgency operation carrying almost no supplies, which almost inevitably turned them into *shifta* in uniform. The system was not only inefficient, it was harmful; the soldiers of the 2d Division, most of whom came from outside Eritrea, tended to behave as occupying forces, further alienating the Eritreans by the use of systematic violence and terrorism.

The Ethiopian armed forces in Eritrea were therefore inefficient, brutal, and corrupt. Their activities lacked planning and coordination. Furthermore, the army was led by generals and colonels who considered military power the only proper way to deal with the Eritrean problem. Whenever the army was given a free hand in the province, the result was a bloody escalation and the crystallization and strengthening of anti-Ethiopian emotions among Eritreans, Christian and Muslim alike.

The only restraining factor was *Ras* Asrate's interest, given his aspirations, in restraining the 2d Division and giving priority in combat activities to "his" commandos and security service, and to the (largely Christian) Eritrean police. Furthermore, it was the *ras*'s consistent policy in Eritrea to use what he termed "constructive means"—that is, intensive propaganda, psychological warfare, and sometimes even direct and quiet negotiations with the separatist organizations. Essentially, he was motivated by the conviction that the Christian Tigreans were to be relied on, encouraged, and trusted (he was a relative and associate of the governor of neighboring Tigre province, *Ras* Mangasha Siyum, a strong believer in the Tigrean contribution to Ethiopian culture and nationalism[8]). Asrate fundamentally distrusted the nomadic Muslims and planned to control them by forcibly resettling them in permanent encampments. In the struggle between *Ras* Asrate and his rivals, notably Prime Minister Aklilu, over Eritrean policy, the latter tended to give the army a free hand. The intensification of terrorist activities and the growing trend among the separatists to execute ever more spectacular acts of sabotage and assassination played into Aklilu's hands, further encouraging a bloody escalation.

Early 1967 brought a quantum leap in the rebels' terrorist activities. In March, a high official was assassinated in the heart of Asmara; this was followed by the killing of an army colonel in Agordat.[9] Subsequently, the army, for the first time, was allowed freedom of action in the Muslim-populated western regions, and its "pacification campaign" brought burning villages, massive aerial bombardments, and brutal massacres throughout the districts between Keren and the Sudanese border.[10] Tens of thousands of refugees fled into the Sudan.[11] The scorched earth campaign that followed was aimed at forcing Muslim nomads to settle in "fortified villages" of some three thousand inhabitants each.[12] (It was after this campaign that *Dadjazmach* Tedla Bairu, former leader of the UP and a leading advocate of a pro-Ethiopian orientation among Tigrean Christians, joined the separatists.)

Asrate, who saw Islam as the main enemy of Ethiopian nationalism, seems to have initiated the anti-Muslim campaign. He had long tried to orient Ethiopia's regional policy on Israel, and Israeli advisers were almost permanent guests in his Asmara palace.[13] Israel's victory in the Six Day War contributed significantly to Asrate's growing influence. Following his advice, the emperor consented to a more flexible policy in troubled Eritrea. A general amnesty was proclaimed, Christian Tigreans considered loyal to the government were armed, and Asrate met with religious functionaries to persuade them to encourage their followers to cooperate with the government.[14] "The emphasis on good will," wrote a Western observer, "is a departure from previous government policy, which had neglected the propaganda aspects of the struggle with the rebels while concentrating on military activities."[15] By the end of 1967, some one hundred rebels, including an important Christian military leader, had surrendered.[16]

Throughout 1968 the Ethiopian authorities maintained full control of the urban centers and the roads between them. On 6 September 1968, when the separatists of region II tried for the first time to capture an Ethiopian army camp at nearby Keren, their forces were crushed, and their commander, Umar Azaz, was killed.[17] Yet it was a turning point militarily, for from late 1968 on, the rebels, better supplied and better trained than before, increasingly took the initiative. Motivated by the competition created by their own splits and rivalries, which drove them to try ever more spectacular acts of assassination, air piracy, kidnapping, dynamiting of bridges, and the like, the Eritreans intensified their activities throughout 1969.[18] By the year's end, Aklilu and his associates were in a position to convince Haile Selassie that Asrate and his Eritrean administration were preventing the army from coping more successfully with the rebels. Ergetu Tshome, the commander of the army in Eritrea, demanded a free hand in the province. On 30 January 1970, prominent ministers and army commanders held a war council.[19]

During the meeting (which was attended by the emperor) or as a result of it, *Ras* Asrate tried to persuade Haile Selassie not to declare martial law in the province and not to let the army pacify Eritrea in its own way. He was, however, unsuccessful, and a carefully planned, wide-scale military offensive started in March with the aim of defeating the rebels around Keren, the coast, and the Sahil. At the same time, Asrate and his advisers tried to reach a territorial compromise with the General Command and Idris Adam. But on 14 April 1970, while the military operation was still in its preliminary stages, the assassination in Asmara of the two Ethiopian judges by Isayas Afawarq gave the hard-liners a golden opportunity. On hearing the news, the emperor authorized Maj. Gen. Ergetu Tshome to act without consulting the governor-general. In response, the frustrated Asrate left for a visit to London. His deputy, Tesfa-Yohannes Berhe, hastened to the capital, where he was coldly received by Haile Selassie. Meanwhile the army, reinforced by new elements from the 1st Division, started an extensive campaign to pacify the regions of Keren, the Sahil, and the coast by burning villages and massacring the population.[20] This campaign, which continued until the beginning of the rainy season in July, coincided with the return from the Adobha meeting of the fighters of the defunct Tripartite Union, the establishment of the PLF (June), and the beginning of the activities of Isayas Afawarq's men, who did their utmost to retaliate and even take the initiative in the brutal struggle.[21]

Meanwhile, the political struggle in Addis Ababa was coming to an end. In early October 1970, the Shoan nobility managed to score an impressive victory over Prime Minister Aklilu and his associates. Chief of Staff Assefa Ayene, who was close to Aklilu, was sent abroad, and in his absence the emperor appointed officers considered to be affiliated with the Shoan nobility to many key military functions. But Asrate was not to savor his success for long; the reality of Ethiopian politics was such that the pendulum of *shum shir* controlled by the emperor would now almost inevitably swing in the opposite direction. Aklilu soon found the proper moment to approach the emperor. In October and November 1970 the situation in Eritrea was deteriorating daily due to rebel initiatives. Five bridges were blown up, and in one case—the explosion of a bridge on the Asmara-Keren road—photographs of the event brought worldwide publicity to the Eritrean camp.[22] Then, on 21 November 1970, Maj. Gen. Ergetu Tshome, the commander of the armed forces in Eritrea, was assassinated by Isayas's men in a carefully executed ambush on the same road.[23] The hard-liners in the capital now gained ascendancy, and the army was given a free hand to "clean" the road between Asmara and Keren. Asrate hastened to Addis Ababa and threatened to resign, but Haile Selassie, following the advice of Aklilu and the army commanders in Eritrea, simply removed him from his position as governor-general of the province. On 16 December 1970, martial law was proclaimed in Eritrea, and the commander of the ground forces, Lt. Gen. Dabbab Haila-Mariam, was appointed military governor. The Eritrean police and the Eritrean commando force that Asrate had established were no longer to be used in major operations. The Eritrean chief of police, Col. Goitem Gabra-Egzi, was transferred to another province. A 10-kilometer strip along the Sudanese border and the Red Sea coast was proclaimed a restricted area, and the army was allowed to solve the Eritrean problem in its own way. Bloody escalation was inevitable.[24]

In retrospect, *Ras* Asrate's removal from his power base in Eritrea was an important event in the contemporary history of Ethiopia. While he was in charge of the province, the regime's approach to the Eritrean problem was much more effective than in later years. But for the continuous outside support to the rebels and undermining activities on the part of his rivals in Ethiopia, his policy—which was a mixture of charitable paternalism to the Christian community and harsh reprisals against individuals—might have been successful. Following his dismissal, Asrate was appointed head of the Crown Council, but after late 1972 his power diminished considerably. Consequently, he spent most of the crucial years of 1973 and early 1974 in London (in the company of the now ailing crown prince), and his attempts to persuade Haile Selassie to abdicate or at least start transferring power to his heir proved futile. Under the growing influence of Aklilu, Haile Selassie continued to lead his country toward instability and chaos.

At the same time, 1972 and 1973 were years of growing rebel weakness for two reasons: the fratricidal war between the ELF-RC and the EPLF and the cessation of Sudanese and Chinese aid in early 1972. The latter was due to Haile Selassie's farsighted and pragmatic international diplomacy.[25] In consequence, the Ethiopian army regained control over the major roads, and the Eritrean separatists had to confine themselves to meaningless and sporadic hit-and-run operations.

Yet the imperial government did nothing of substance to cope with the Eritrean problem; once again, it was officially ignored.[26] In practice, under the military government the province became more and more an occupied territory. Christian Tigreans, the majority of whom had identified with Ethiopia during Asrate's rule and had served in the Eritrean police and the other units, were gradually antagonized by the army's systematic brutality. As we shall see, during the revolution of 1974 and after, Eritrean Christians identified strongly with Eritrean nationalism. This was due, in no small part, to the Ethiopian policy of martial law instituted in 1970.

4.   Eritrea and the
1974 Revolution in Ethiopia

The fall of Haile Selassie's regime in Ethiopia and the assumption of power by young officers of the same generation as the Eritrean field commanders did nothing to improve the situation in Eritrea. Instead, the end of 1974 saw the outbreak of open, conventional war.

This was a sharp contrast to the immediately preceding period. In 1973 and the first half of 1974, the Eritrean resistance to the Ethiopian army had been quite passive—partly because the province was famine stricken and partly because the ELF-RC and EPLF were preoccupied with fighting each other. With assassinations, ambushes, and kidnappings only sporadic,[1] the Eritrean-based Ethiopian army units had been left relatively free and were able to play an important role in the making of their country's revolution.

In retrospect, it would seem that the events of 1974 resulted from the spontaneous emergence of a strong protest movement rather than a planned revolution.[2] By as early as February, the protest movement was strong enough in the armed forces to virtually destroy the already decrepit political establishment, which had slowly paralyzed itself throughout the early 1970s as it focused on the machinations of the increasingly senile absolutist. The members of the establishment had concentrated on preparations for the future struggle for power and ignored the acute challenges facing their people—famine, inflation, the growing ideological crisis. Many were simply blind to the emerging realities; others were aware of the stagnation but too dependent on the emperor's favor to initiate change.

The problem was particularly acute in the army. Ethiopian officers from the rank of lieutenant colonel up were generally members of the ruling establishment and enjoyed high salaries while often exploiting their soldiers by selling them food and other necessities. The gap between the colonels and generals and those below them was especially wide in Eritrea, where, in addition to their regular grievances, the rank and file, NCOs, and young officers had to bear the brunt of the actual fighting. Under the circumstances, it was hardly surprising that a protest movement developed in the army and led, in February 1974, to the arrest of many colonels and generals by soldiers, NCOs, and junior officers. One reason why the protest movement of Eritrean soldiers proved so effective was because those units whose loyalty to the old commanders was most certain, such as the Airborne Brigade, were posted in far-off Addis Ababa and its environs. Another factor was that by 1974 the majority of the Eritrean-recruited police and commandos tacitly sided with the Eritrean cause and were thus active participants in the protest movement. Moreover, the Eritrean-based army officers must have been frustrated because the breaking of diplomatic relations with Israel in October 1973 meant the departure of their tactical advisers.

The mutiny in the Eritrean-based units started, as in the other units of the Ethiopian army, during February 1974. By 24 February the majority of high-ranking officers were behind bars; the rest resigned themselves to passivity, while the soldiers, led by NCOs and low-ranking officers, took control of Asmara and the airport.

The emperor's aide-de-camp, Maj. Gen. Assefa Demise, was sent from the capital with a small military delegation in an attempt to come to terms with the rebellious troops. The members of the delegation were arrested, but Assefa Demise was permitted to meet with Eritrea's military governor, Lt. Gen. Dabbab Haila-Mariam, and with representatives of the mutineers. He returned to the capital with a letter containing the soldiers' demands: higher pay for enlisted men; better compensation for loss of life or limb; a narrowing in the differential in pay and conditions between officers and other ranks; improvement in uniforms; better pensions; and the cessation of the use of private soldiers as officers' gardeners and house servants. The soldiers also condemned the large salaries and expense accounts of ministers and high officials and demanded that officials pay for their own Mercedes cars.[3]

On returning to Addis Ababa, Assefa Demise met with members of a committee representing the capital-based mutineers, who presented him with a similar list. These demands, coupled with intensive civilian rioting and the organization by young officers and NCOs of committees to assume control of the various battalions, brought about the fall of Aklilu's government on 27 February. The success of the protest movement meant the collapse of the regime. Since the protesting factions were neither ready nor able to start building a new order, the Shoan nobility group headed by *Ras* Asrate Kassa was asked to retain control temporarily. However, in late June, the creation of the Derg channeled the protest into revolution.

Aklilu's resignation thus proved to be a sweet but temporary triumph for the Shoan nobility group. The leader of the Addis Ababa committee at the time was the commander of the Airborne Brigade, Col. Alam-Zawd Tasamma, a close associate and relative by marriage of a prominent member of the Shoan nobility group, Endalkatchaw Makonnen. Assefa Demise was also affiliated with the Shoan nobility, as was Dabbab Haila-Mariam, Eritrea's military governor. These three officers, with Assefa Demise presenting the mutineers' demands to the emperor, managed to put their group at the head of the protest movement.[4] They simply told Haile Selassie that the army wanted Endalkatchaw as prime minister, and the now powerless emperor had no alternative but to appoint him. Abiy Ababa, another Shoan noble, was appointed defense minister, and Col. Alam-Zawd Tasamma constituted the new government's source of military support. *Ras* Asrate remained in the background, biding his time and awaiting Endalkatchaw's downfall. Aklilu and his ministers were promptly imprisoned to await investigation and trial. In Eritrea, Dabbab Haila-Mariam managed temporarily to convince the mutineers that they had scored an impressive victory; and indeed, on 1 March 1974, the soldiers in Asmara used the captured radio station to broadcast a request for calm in the rest of the army.

The victory of the Shoan nobility was short-lived. While the new government tried to rely on Alam-Zawd and his paratroopers, the protest movement in the army's various units was growing stronger and becoming increasingly politicized. Revolutionary officers were taking over the committees in the various battalions all over the country, and students and other sectors of the civilian population continued to demonstrate and strike. A government headed by Shoan nobles was seen as little more than a cosmetic change incompatible with the growing politicization of the protest movement in the army and in the civilian sector.

The major political process leading to the expected revolutionary change took place in and around Addis Ababa, culminating in June with the establishment of the Derg. Meanwhile, the revolutionaries in the capital were facing units loyal to the government, notably paratroopers under Alam-Zawd. After 24 March 1974, for instance, these paratroopers, having arrested many revolutionary mutineers, were in control of the Dabra-Zait air base near Addis Ababa, where the revolutionaries had their headquarters. In far-off Asmara, however, the revolutionaries took over with little opposition. By the end of March, a committee representing "the Armed Forces of the North," made up of members of the 2d Division, the police, the commando forces, the air force, and the navy, had been formed in Asmara. On 26 March, reacting to the occupation of Dabra-Zait by Alam-Zawd's troops, the Armed Forces of the North temporarily seized control of the Asmara airport again, arrested Dabbab Haila-Mariam, the police commissioner, and the commander of the 2d Division (all of whom were soon freed), and demanded the release of their fellow revolutionaries held in the capital. They also demanded that Endalkatchaw be tried for corruption and that the ELF be legalized (this last at the demand of the commandos and police).[5] Throughout April, May, and June, the administration of the country verged on chaos. The Eritrean police went on strike on 19 April, and other sectors soon followed.[6]

These developments in Eritrea had some effect on events in Addis Ababa, where in June the protest movement was channeled into a revolution with the formation of the Coordinating Committee of the Armed Forces, otherwise known as the Derg. Later the same month, the Derg took control of the capital and arrested all prominent members of the Shoan nobility group—*Ras* Asrate and Abiy in late June and Endalkatchaw in late July. Simultaneously the Armed Forces Committee of the North arrested the leading figures in the Eritrean administration—notably, on 17 July, Lt. Gen. Dabbab Haila-Mariam and the mayor of Asmara, *Dadjazmach* Haragot Abbay.[7] Representatives of this committee had joined the Derg, the new ruling body of Ethiopia, early in July 1974, and this led to the arrest of all the leading politicians, generals, and other members of Haile Selassie's establishment. This smoothly executed "creeping coup" culminated on 12 September with a humiliating deposition ceremony ending Haile Selassie's emperorship.

The establishment of the Derg did not signify the emergence of a new leadership. The new ruling body, which consisted of some 120 young soldiers, was essentially the product of a spontaneous process, and it consequently lacked both internal cohesion and experience. Its membership comprised three representatives of each of the 36 battalions of the armed services, police, and other armed forces, as well as military academies and other units. Battalion commanders and higher officers were excluded by definition; over half the delegates were NCOs and privates. The authoritative centralism of Haile Selassie was replaced by a collegial body in which the decision-making process necessitated a certain consensus.

The main reason for this need for consensus arose because at least during the first two years after the Derg's establishment, no member could muster the support of a military unit stronger than that his colleagues could muster. Decisions on major issues had to be reached through debate and intrigue, which determined not only the making of policy, but also guaranteed a merciless elimination process in the internal contest for power. At the same time, the struggle for power among the more ambitious members was naturally a major factor influencing policymaking. As in the past, the Eritrean issue played an important role in the internal competition and was itself affected by the process. Unfortunately, as in the recent past, the hard-liners in the Eritrean camp consistently played into the hands of the hard-liners in the new ruling body. Tragically for Eritrea, both sides would emerge victorious.

In the sphere of ideology, as in other fields, the Derg started off very cautiously. Till the end of 1974, it acted under the catchall slogan of "Ethiopia Tiqdam," officially translated as "Ethiopia First." During the gradual destruction of the old order, some of the social and economic aspects of the slogan were clarified. On 20 December 1974, Ethiopian socialism was declared and a policy of nationalization that culminated in March 1975 with a radical declaration on land reform was initiated. The new orientation to socialism would later prove of much significance to the Eritrean problem. What was of immediate importance, however, was the nationalist significance of the slogan. Here consensus had prevailed from the start: the concept of territorial nationalism was to remain intact. Every member denied the legitimacy of any claim to the right of self-determination by ethnic, linguistic, and provincial groups. Like the constitutions of 1955 and 1931, the official declaration of 20 December 1974 opened with a definition of Ethiopia that clearly included Eritrea.[8]

The Derg's arguments and struggles over Eritrea had little to do with ideology or theory. The points of difference lay in the sphere of practice and over the question of how to fight the separatists. As in the Asrate-Aklilu period, the differences were substantive.

During the first half of 1974, no one in the capital had either the time or the power to conduct an Eritrean policy. All energies were devoted to the struggle for survival. For instance, *Dadjazmach* Dr. Zawde Gabra-Sellasse, minister of interior in Endalkatchaw's government, a historian, and a devoted liberal, was a dedicated pursuer of a political solution in Eritrea; yet his initiatives (including the abolition of the military government in Eritrea and frequent consultations with the 23 Eritrean members of parliament) proved fruitless, for the government was powerless.[9] Only with the formation of the Derg in July did a body capable of conducting any policy emerge in the capital.

By that time, however, the Eritrean question had gone beyond the bounds of manageability. Between February and May 1974, both the ELF-RC and the EPLF had avoided attacking the army. Instead, they went on fighting each other and executing minor terrorist activities. Some Eritrean leaders thought that the revolution was weakening the Ethiopians and that an attack might have the effect of unifying their torn army.[10] Another probable reason for this grace period was that some members of the Armed Forces Committee of the North, especially representatives of the police, were already in touch with their fellow Christian Tigreans in the EPLF. During June, however, a wave of terrorist activities and assassinations swept the province. On 20 June, the mounting campaign of terror reached Asmara; eight people were killed when a bomb was detonated beneath a bus, and a gunman shot and killed *Ato* Ibrahim

Hamid Aray, a prominent adviser to the governor-general. The next day, the guerrillas executed five policemen near Asmara.[11] Then, in the second week of July, *Dadjazmach* Hamid Faraj Hamid, former president of the Eritrean assembly during the federation and later a member of Asrate's "cabinet," was assassinated in Agordat, reportedly for advocating a federative solution.[12] Immediately afterward, the Ethiopian colonel in command of the brigade posted in western Eritrea was assassinated in the town of Um Hager.

The Ethiopian army, for its part, contributed heavily to the escalation. In late July, the officers and soldiers of the western brigade revenged their assassinated commander in a brutal massacre at Um Hager. Some two hundred citizens were reported slain, and an estimated four thousand people fled to the Sudan.

Simultaneously, the war of declarations was resumed. Uthman Sabi stated in early June: "Perhaps the Ethiopian government is thinking of coming out with a kind of middle solution like the restoration of the federation or granting a kind of an autonomy to Eritrea. But the Ethiopian government should know that the Eritrean people will not accept less than getting their legitimate rights, that is, full national sovereignty and independence."[13] Late in June, it was revealed in Addis Ababa that the Derg's demand for the release of political prisoners on 3 July had excluded Eritrean prisoners (thought to number several hundred).

In response to the news of the Um Hager massacre and the discrimination against Eritrean prisoners, the 23 Eritrean members of the Ethiopian parliament resigned. Their bitter letter of resignation reflected their growing sympathy for the cause of Eritrean separatism. They condemned the systematic atrocities of the army in Eritrea and complained that "Eritreans who were imprisoned because their feelings for their country were considered a crime" had been denied political amnesty.[14] The resignation of the Eritrean members of parliament put the Eritrean issue on the capital's complex political agenda.

In the meantime a major development had taken place in the Ethiopian political scene. On 3 July 1974, the young officers of the Derg had forced the emperor to appoint Lt. Gen. Aman Mikael Andom as chief of staff. Later, when Endalkatchaw was removed (22 July) and a new government formed by the Derg under *Lij* Mikael Imru, Aman was made minister of defense. With the deposition of Haile Selassie on 12 September, Aman, as chairman of the new ruling body—the Provisional Military Administrative Council (PMAC)—became acting head of state.

Aman Mikael Andom was an Eritrean. He was born in 1924 in the village of Tsazegga, some 25 kilometers north of Asmara.[15] Prior to the establishment of Asmara by *Ras* Alula in 1885, this village had for centuries been the headquarters of a local Christian Tigrean family that succeeded in maintaining its autonomy from the Ethiopian emperors.[16] Educated in Khartoum, Aman returned to Ethiopia in 1941 with the British forces who defeated Mussolini's African empire and restored Haile Selassie to the throne. He proceeded to distinguish himself in a brilliant military career, commanding Ethiopian contingents in Korea and the Congo. In the Ogaden battles against the Somalis in the early 1960s, he willfully ignored Haile Selassie's orders and was consequently "exiled" to the Senate in 1965, as was the practice with overly independent political figures. Yet he maintained close relations with the generals and was among the few high-ranking officers admired by the rank and file. It was for this reason that the architects of the Derg chose him as chairman of the PMAC—despite his well-known pride in his Eritrean background. General Aman was married to a sister of Dr. Biasolo, the mentor and spiritual father of such Eritrean leaders as Isayas Afawarq and Heruy Tedla-Bairu, and was familiar with Eritrean politics, rivalries, and splits. As such, he set as his prime objective a constructive political solution to the Eritrean problem.

On 20 August, the Ethiopian parliament called on its Eritrean members to withdraw their letter of resignation. A speech made by Prime Minister Mikael Imru during the debate was the first in the history of the Eritrean conflict in which an Ethiopian official admitted that a serious problem existed and that the solution lay in political dialogue.[17] Similarly, Minister of Defense Aman Andom declared that solving the Eritrean problem was the nation's top priority and that he would do his utmost to achieve a solution. The next week he left for an extensive tour of the province.

During late August and early September, Aman made public appearances all over Eritrea, addressing packed stadiums in Asmara, Keren, and elsewhere. Speaking in Tigrinya and Arabic,[18] whose use had been officially forbidden, he urged his listeners to blame social, economic, and cultural problems on the defunct regime. He admitted that Ethiopian hard-liners, by resorting exclusively to military power, had encouraged Eritrean separatism; but, at the same time, he emphasized that "Eritrea had been historically an integral part of Ethiopia . . . that the problem of Eritrea is the problem of the entire Ethiopia . . . [and that] we are jealous of our unity."[19]

On 9 September 1974, back in the capital, Aman presented a detailed nineteen-point plan to solve the problem. It called for "general reform of the administrative system, removal of all obstacles which had impeded social progress . . . amnesty of political prisoners in Eritrea, return of exiles and their resettlement, promotion of foreign investments . . . lifting the state of emergency, punishing officials responsible for misconduct in Eritrea," as well as "safeguarding Ethiopian unity."[20]

Beyond the facade of declarations, however, Aman had attempted during his tour to reach an understanding and cooperate with Christian elements in the EPLF. Eritrean policemen were in touch with EPLF fighters, and Aman was himself personally acquainted with some of the separatist leaders. Aman apparently believed that Christian Tigreans in the EPLF would be satisfied with a sort of Eritrean autonomy; according to Zawde Gabra-Sellasse, he thought that they would join hands with the Ethiopian army in a common war against the ELF-RC.[21] Using the services of Sudanese President Numayri, Aman conveyed to some of the Eritrean leaders in exile the idea of an autonomous Eritrean unit linked federally with Ethiopia. As a token of goodwill, for the first time since the federation a Christian Eritrean was appointed Eritrea's governor-general. This was *Ato* Amanuel Amda-Mikael, who, on arriving at Asmara later in September, swore to become Eritrea's servant rather than its governor.[22] Another significant appointment made by Aman was to reinstall Brig. Gen. Goitem Gabra-Egzi, also an Eritrean, as commissioner of the Eritrean police, a position he had held until the removal of Asrate. But Aman's attempt to persuade Eritrean leaders was unsuccessful. Nor was he able to convince his younger colleagues in the Derg that his political approach was justified. This double failure was soon to lead to his political downfall—and to his death.

The first to reject Aman's proposals were Eritrean leaders in exile. Neither Muslims nor Christians, of either organization, left any room for compromise. "This is an unacceptable program," the EPLF spokesman in Rome stated. "We want our old flag back."[23] The Beirut-published EPLF *Eritrean Review* made this quite clear in its September issue. In a late reaction to the Um Hager massacre, it wrote: "Let us bring to the notice of the new rulers of Ethiopia that our military operations will be extended to every span of the Eritrean territory. Then we will see what the Ethiopian colonialist army can do."[24] In the same issue, Muhammad Said Nawud, the EPLF director of central information, reacted to Aman's proposals: "Aman Andom is an Eritrean traitor and a stooge of the Ethiopian government . . . to arrive at a political solution cannot be accomplished by means of sending stooges to Eritrea. This can only be achieved by adopting a clear-cut position recognizing the realities imposed by the Eritrean revolution . . . We are ready to sit with the Ethiopians and negotiate with them on the question of full independence for Eritrea, while at the same time holding our arms in our hands."[25]

Throughout September Aman faced growing opposition in the Derg, while at the same time his policy suffered another blow in the province itself, where the EPLF and ELF-RC were still engaged in their fratricidal war. A core unit of some five hundred EPLF fighters, long besieged near Karora by the ELF-RC, managed to break away and move to the village of Zager, near Asmara, where contact was established with members of the Ethiopian armed forces (who were, most probably, following Aman's instructions in this matter).[26] When the pursuing ELF-RC forces camped at the nearby village of Woki during the first week of October, a major battle ensued between the two Eritrean forces. The battle lasted for a few days and claimed the lives of some six hundred fighters.[27] It ended in a most peculiar way, becoming a milestone in the history of the Eritrean nationalist movement. When news of the battle reached Asmara, some fifty thousand citizens left the town, reputedly at the urging of Aman's men and made their way to the site of the battle.[28] By that time many fighters had ceased firing, refusing to shoot at fellow Eritreans. A mass rally was spontaneously organized at Woki, and under the pressure of this popular demonstration and manifestation of Eritrean patriotism, the warring units reached an agreement.[29] Nothing was concluded in writing concerning actual cooperation between the rival parties, but in retrospect it was a spectacular end to Eritrea's fratricidal war. The rally took on a strongly anti-Ethiopian character, a clear demonstration that the majority of Christian Eritreans looked to the separatist organizations for leadership.

The rally at Woki caused deep frustration among Ethiopian officers of the 2d Division. Their new commander, Brig. Gen. Tafari Banti, who had been appointed in September 1974,[30] was of Oromo origin (like many other members of the Derg) and was known as a hard-liner on Eritrea. Following the rally, he asked the Derg for authorization to open war on the rebels and demanded reinforcements from the capital. His request was favorably received by the Derg's young vice-chairman, Maj. Mangistu Haila-Mariam. Mangistu, who was already building a strong position in the Derg that would undermine Aman, had been one of Tafari's cadets at the military academy and was himself a hard-liner. Mangistu's response both infuriated and frustrated Aman. His position in the Derg had become precarious since Tafari Banti's appointment and that of a new chief of staff had been confirmed by the Derg despite his opposition. In an effort to save his position and his policy, Aman managed to prevent a decision to send reinforcements to Eritrea; instead, he left for the province on 6 October 1974. There he succeeded in restraining the commanders of the 2d Division. Addressing a mass rally in the central stadium, Aman urged the thousands who had just demonstrated their Eritreanism at Woki to consider the opportunities they had been given. If the chances presented by his program were missed, forcing Ethiopia's rulers to take retaliatory measures, the people should be aware of the possible consequences. It appeared, Aman went on bitterly, that the people of Eritrea had not grasped the aims and objectives of the movement and the administrative reforms Addis Ababa envisaged for Eritrea. "You have been given opportunities," he concluded. "Consider them carefully. 'Ethiopia Tikdem' is based on Ethiopian unity. All of us, from all the 14 administrative regions of the country, should strive in unity to advance Ethiopia to the standard of other countries."[31]

Aman returned to Addis Ababa on the same day. The people of Asmara gave him their reply a week later. On 13 October, representatives of the EPLF and ELF-RC, as well as some twenty to thirty thousand citizens, attended another rally, held just outside the town.[32] The army, though still restrained, started demonstrating its presence in and around the town. Uthman Sabi, with perfect timing, declared that the separatists, now stronger than ever, were about to initiate a new stage in the war against the Ethiopians. No more hit-and-run operations, he promised. The Eritrean organizations would launch offensives against the army in its own camps and transfer the battle to the main towns. Furthermore, the Eritreans would encourage other minority groups in Ethiopia itself in order to encourage anarchy there.[33]

The victory of the uncompromising sectors in the Eritrean camp signaled that Aman's end was approaching and that the Ethiopian hard-liners would emerge victorious. Aman's influence in the Derg rested on the support of a few members, mainly the representatives of the Imperial Guard (1st Division) and of the Addis Ababa police; he had not been a real factor in the making of the protest movement or in the establishment of the Derg. Although in close touch with some of the revolutionaries in the early stages, he was chosen as chief of staff and chairman of the PMAC essentially because of his popularity and his image as an opponent of the emperor. Aman, however, refused to confine himself to being a mere figurehead. He was confident that his charisma could not fail him and that he was the real guide of the youngsters in the Derg. Without bothering too much about his power base in the ruling body, Aman tried to direct the revolution according to his concepts. In his public appearances as acting head of state, Aman tried to restrain expectations for prompt and drastic changes. He supported gradual land reform and foreign investment and opposed spectacular nationalizations. He resisted both the Marxist-oriented officers who favored the immediate transfer of rule to civilians and others who wished to prolong military rule. He also opposed such ideas as the instant execution of arrested officials and established special courts to hold proper trials. All this created a gap between the patronizing and proud Aman and the core group in the Derg of mid-level officers led by Major Mangistu. But it was primarily over the Eritrean issue that differences between Aman and the younger officers turned into conflict. While Tafari Banti in Eritrea was demanding reinforcements for an extensive military campaign, Major Mangistu in the Derg was pushing for a decision to let the army take the initiative against the rebels. Although Aman could offer no proof of the success of his own policy, he firmly resisted the move. An important and related matter was that the troops designated for the Eritrean campaign were some five thousand members of the 1st Division, known to support Aman's few followers in the Derg.[34] Their removal from Addis Ababa would further undermine Aman's power base.

The struggle between Mangistu and Aman broke into the open in the second week of November, when both leaders were touring army bases making contradictory statements. Mangistu, reverting to the tactic of ignoring the Eritrean situation, referred to "the few guerrillas who had been maintaining a state of insecurity in the region for the last 13 years, with the collaboration of foreign countries."[35]

Aman stood no chance of winning the struggle in the Derg because he was an outsider, while Mangistu enjoyed the support of many of the NCOs and some of the officers. The majority of these NCOs were of Oromo origin, and they probably suspected Aman, on the basis of his origin, of being too tolerant of Eritreanism. Aman's only chance was to mobilize support outside the Derg, mainly of some units of the Harar-based 3rd Division, but despite his associates' advice, the overconfident Aman refused to start an open war.[36] Instead, on 15 November he proudly confined himself to his Addis Ababa house and waited for the youngsters of the Derg to come and beg him to return. On 23 November, the Derg sent troops to arrest him, and in the ensuing gunfight, he and two of his associates were killed. On the same night, 57 of the officials arrested since the start of the revolution were executed without trial. Among them were almost all important figures in Ethiopian politics during the period so far discussed (with the exception of the emperor, who died in August 1975[37]), including Asrate, Aklilu, Endalkatchaw, and Dabbab Haila-Mariam. The Derg ordered 5,000 soldiers of the 1st Division to move to Eritrea and reinforce the army there in preparation for a military confrontation with the separatists.

In the Eritrean context, Aman's defeat by Mangistu resembled that of Asrate by Aklilu. Both Aman and Asrate were working for a political solution, pinning their hopes on the Christian Tigrean community in Eritrea. Asrate failed primarily because he ignored the Muslims and because as a representative of conservative absolutism, he could not attract the emerging generation of educated Christians. Aman, representing a new Ethiopia, came too late in the Eritrean context. By the time he appeared, Ethiopian hard-liners had seen to it that Christian Eritreans identified Ethiopia with systematic brutality. "Twenty years ago," a prominent Christian leader in Asmara was quoted as saying, "I favored union. I was one of those shouting 'Unity or Death.' What we got was Ethiopia and death."[38] Both Aman and Asrate, however, were given little opportunity to implement their policies. In 1974, as in 1970, hard-liners on both sides prevented a political solution in the war-torn province.

With the fall of Aman Andom, the outbreak of conventional, open war in Eritrea became inevitable. All hopes that a new regime in Ethiopia would lead to a peaceful solution were shattered. By the time of the Ethiopian revolution of 1974, the nucleus of a nationalist movement had emerged in Eritrea. The revolution, inasmuch as it weakened the Ethiopian state machinery, raised nationalist expectations among the Eritreans. The uncompromising policy that the Derg adopted after Aman died served only to strengthen the rapidly growing Eritrean movement. At the same time the unstable situation in

Ethiopia encouraged Arab support for the Eritreans, with obvious implications on the battlefield.

The Eritreans were the first to take the military initiative. Reacting to the arrival of Ethiopian reinforcements, the rebels carried the battle into the heart of Asmara. On 22 December 1974, hundreds of guerrillas infiltrated the town, and clashes with civilians claimed the lives of twelve citizens.[39] The army reacted accordingly, and violent activities in and around the town intensified.

The Ethiopian Derg was now a war council. Tafari Banti was recalled from Eritrea and appointed chairman of PMAC and acting head of state. Official announcements to Eritreans were harshly phrased.[40] "What is the use of patience?" said a statement reflecting the general mood in the Derg. "We must change our peaceful attitude."[41]

The Derg was making a last effort to gain time and possibly to deter Arab countries from sending aid to the rebels. On 28 December, a mission headed by ex–Prime Minister Mikael Imru (now chief political adviser) and Mangistu's associate and Derg member Maj. Berhanu Bayeh left for Asmara, where a group of 345 Eritrean dignitaries was assembled. Instead of listening to the officials, the Eritreans expressed their own minds: "Haile Selassie tried to destroy Eritrea," the prior of the nearby Debra-Bizan monastery, an ancient citadel of Ethiopian Christianity, said. "Now the army is trying to do the same, but will not succeed. I speak frankly as I am old and not afraid to die tomorrow."[42] The consensus among the dignitaries was that negotiations concerning the future of Eritrea had to be conducted with the Eritrean organizations. A committee of 38 members formed on the spot was authorized to establish contact with the rebels. Four of its members were later reported to have established such contacts,[43] yet nothing of significance came of the whole affair.

By this time, however, the Eritreans were voting with their feet. Thousands were leaving Asmara and joining the rebel organizations. In early January, Police Commissioner Brig. Gen. Goitem Gabra-Egzi led many of his men to join the swelling camps of the Eritreans. They were followed by some members of the Massawa-based navy.[44] The mass exodus from Asmara brought increased popular pressure for a reconciliation between the ELF-RC and the EPLF. On 31 January 1975 in Koazien, under pressure from Goitem Gabra-Egzi and others, the two organizations concluded a military agreement.[45] At the same time, the Derg officially declared war.[46]

5. The Middle East and Eritrea, 1962–1974

The struggle over Eritrea and the Horn of Africa should be viewed as an integral part of Red Sea and Middle Eastern affairs rather than as an African conflict. By the 1980s, such an assertion would seem to be dwelling on the obvious. All local actors in the Eritrean conflict (or in other major issues concerning the Horn of Africa) are directly connected, sometimes even closely allied, with Middle Eastern countries and organizations. Against the background of the more distant past, however, this is a significant innovation. Understanding this change in context is essential for a proper assessment of the Eritrean conflict.

Throughout history, the Arabs and Muslims of the Middle East neglected the African coast of the Red Sea. The medieval Arabs who established the Middle Eastern and North African Muslim empires conceived the Red Sea as a natural boundary. Their Turkish successors, more able in naval warfare, tried to control the Red Sea and establish a foothold along its African coast, but they failed and abandoned the idea. Consequently Middle Eastern Muslims (and later in the twentieth century, the leaders of Arab states) were indifferent to their coreligionists in the Horn of Africa. This was a major reason for Ethiopia's historical political hegemony in the Horn—local Muslims were unable to unite against the Christian domination.

Modern Eritrean separatism played a significant role in bridging the Red Sea and connecting the Horn with the Middle East. It started as a movement uniting Eritrean Muslims and developed into an Eritrean nationalist movement, which some of its leaders saw as an Arab movement. In the 1960s the fulfillment of Eritrean nationalism became a strategic and ideological goal for many Middle Eastern Arab states. For the same reason, Israel conceived Eritrean separatism as a potential threat to its strategic interests in the Red Sea. From the early 1960s on, events in the Horn began to arouse interest throughout the Middle East. Since the Ethiopian revolution resulted in the weakening of Ethiopia and the strengthening of the Eritrean movement, it marked the beginning of an all-Arab consensus concerning the strategic importance of the Red Sea, whose future role was dubbed that of an "Arab lake." This had considerable implications for the Arab attitude toward Eritrean nationalism.

Such a consensus had not existed before the 1974 revolution. As long as Ethiopia was militarily strong and diplomatically influential, the attitudes of Arab states toward the Eritrean question depended largely on their location. States lying away from the Red Sea and thus not exposed to Ethiopia's military or diplomatic might could afford to indulge in full ideological identification with the Eritreans and extend them material support. This was true of Syria, Iraq, Algeria, and Libya, as well as the PLO. Among the Red Sea Arab states, in contrast, the Eritreans found support only from the People's Democratic Republic of Yemen (PDRY). These supporters of the Eritreans were, it is reasonable to assume, also working in the service of the Soviet Union; in some instances the arms they supplied to the Eritreans had been received, at little or no cost, from the Soviet Union or other communist countries. Since most of the pro-Eritrean states lay far from the battlefield, their moral and material aid could not be a decisive factor in resolving the conflict. Support for the guerrillas enhanced their nuisance value, but was insufficient to turn them into a force capable of defeating the Ethiopian army.

Most of the Arab states closer to Ethiopia—the states bordering the Red Sea or Ethiopia itself, whose support for the Eritreans could have been far more meaningful—adopted a pragmatic and therefore ambivalent attitude toward the Eritrean problem and avoided giving the rebels significant support. These states included Egypt, the Sudan, Saudi Arabia, and Somalia. Efforts by Eritrean leaders to obtain their full and consistent support proved fruitless. Even their claim that they were struggling against an ally of Israel was insufficient; Ethiopia at the time was simply too strong to be challenged by its Red Sea neighbors. Only when Ethiopia had been weakened by the revolution did the neighboring Arab countries adopt a posture of confrontaton, and this happened even though Ethiopia had by now severed diplomatic relations with Israel. In 1977, when revolutionary Ethiopia allied itself with the Soviet Union, Arab opposition was indicated by the call to Arabize the Red Sea.

But until the 1974 revolution, Ethiopia—supported by the United States and other Western countries—was militarily strong and diplomatically influential. Its regional ally was Israel. The cooperation and understanding between the two states stemmed not only from the traditional Ethiopian attitude toward the Bible and Israel, but also from sharing a common enemy: Pan-Arabism—that is, the tendency of Middle Eastern Arabs to conceive the Middle East (including, by this time, the west coast of the Red Sea) as an Arab world and to strive to fulfill this ideal at the expense of the nationalist rights of non-Arabs.

The Ethiopian-Israeli alliance started in 1958, the year in which Pan-Arabism reached its zenith in the establishment of the United Arab Republic (UAR). Israel's reaction, initiated by Prime Minister David Ben-Gurion, was to try to ally itself with the pro-Western, non-Arab countries peripheral to the Middle East—Turkey, Iran, and Ethiopia. Israeli support for Ethiopia was rendered in various fields, but was quantitatively far less than that of some other Western countries. Even at the height of their relations in the late 1960s (after the Six Day War) and the early 1970s, the number of Israelis in Ethiopia—army and police officers, experts in the fields of agriculture, education, transportation, health, industry, banking, and urban planning—never exceeded one hundred. The Israelis, however, enjoyed the confidence and trust of their hosts and proved to be efficient and reliable.

An important example of this was Israel's role in saving Haile Selassie during the abortive coup of December 1960.[1] The emperor was touring Brazil when mutineers took over in Addis Ababa. Following the explicit instructions of Prime Minister Ben-Gurion and Foreign Minister Golda Meir, the Israelis helped the emperor establish contact with his followers, notably Abiy Ababa (then the *enderase* in Eritrea) and Asrate Kassa, who led the campaign to quell the coup.

In September 1961, following the dismemberment of the UAR, Ben-Gurion felt confident enough to demand the establishment of diplomatic relations between the two countries.[2] Israel opened an embassy in Addis Ababa, but Haile Selassie kept official relations at a low profile; the Ethiopians opened only a consulate in Jerusalem, and Israeli officers training Ethiopian units were requested not to appear in uniform on official occasions.[3] In practice, however, relations between the two countries continued to flourish. Economic and cultural relations were remarkably strong and of much mutual benefit. Units of the Ethiopian army and other branches of the security forces were trained by members of the Israeli military delegation. Their involvement included instruction at the army's Staff College at Holeta and participation in general planning and training.[4]

In 1969 Israel suggested that Ethiopia and Israel, with Turkey and Iran, sign a formal treaty of alliance.[5] Officially, the Ethiopians shelved the idea, but in practice relations had already reached this level. In the Red Sea, the two countries' common interest was obvious: to prevent the establishment of an independent Eritrea. Israeli opposition was based on the probable affiliation of Eritrean leaders with Arabism and the PLO. Consequently, Israel's influence iopia was strengthened as Syrian, Iraqi, Libyan, Sudanese, and PLO support for the Eritrean separatists increased. According to a persistent allegation by the Eritreans (equally persistently denied by the Israelis), Israel even had a naval presence in some tiny Ethiopian islands near the Eritrean coast and the strait of Bab al-Mandab.[6]

On the Ethiopian side, the most prominent advocate of cooperation with Israel was *Ras* Asrate Kassa. He saw Israel as Ethiopia's main ally and conceived the emerging Pan-Arabism and the politicization of Islam in the Horn of Africa as a grave threat. Ethiopia's positive orientation toward Israel began with Asrate's appointment as *enderase* in Eritrea in 1964. From then on, Israel maintained a presence in Eritrea of some ten to twelve advisers on counterinsurgency, who were closely associated with the *ras*. Beginning in 1964, the Israelis were in charge of building, training, and supplying the locally recruited forces that Asrate was working to strengthen—namely, the commandos and the police. Some of the Christian Eritrean commando officers were even sent to Israel for advanced training.[7] The Israeli advisers' position in the U.S.-trained and supplied 2d Division, on the other hand, was minimal. Their efforts to promote the formation of a joint command to coordinate activities against the separatists, to restrain the army, and to make it answerable to the *ras* proved fruitless. The Israelis had to watch from a distance while the violence of the Ethiopian army played into the hands of the ELF. As the frustrated head of the Israeli military delegation told his colleagues in late April 1967, "The 2d Division is very efficient in killing innocent people. They are alienating the Eritreans and deepening the hatred that already exists. Their commander took his senior aides to a spot near the Sudanese border and ordered them: 'From here to the north—clean the area.' Many innocent people were massacred and nothing of substance was achieved. There is simply no way the Ethiopian army will ever win the struggle over Eritrea by pursuing this line."[8]

Asrate's archrival in Ethiopian politics, Prime Minister Aklilu, was of a different regional orientation. Aklilu conceived Ethiopia's alliance with Israel as unnecessary provocation of the Arabs. His victory over Asrate on the Eritrean issue and Asrate's consequent weakened position were heavy blows to Israel's influence. The army now followed the central government's (Aklilu's) line in Eritrea, and the role of the commandos and police, with their Israeli advisers and trainers, was considerably diminished. As the old monarch grew less interested in his country's internal problems and more inclined toward the prestige of diplomacy, Aklilu's influence increased. Moreover, the growing weight of the Arab and Muslim lobby in Addis Ababa eroded Israel's position. In early 1972, Haile Selassie scored a significant diplomatic achievement in Eritrea when he signed an agreement with neighboring Sudan (see below). Influenced by Aklilu he apparently believed that the way to solve the Eritrean problem was to use diplomacy to appease Eritrea's Arab supporters and use the army to crush the separatist organizations. Israel remained important only as a pro-Ethiopian advocate in Washington whenever it came to asking for U.S. aid and arms.[9] In other respects, Israel was fast losing ground.

At a conference of the Organization of African Unity (OAU) in Addis Ababa in May 1973, Ethiopia came under heavy pressure, especially from Libya, to break relations with Israel. Promises and threats by other Arab countries, notably Saudi Arabia, followed.[10] Aklilu, too, persistently pushed the emperor to sever relations. The Yom Kippur War saw the collapse of Israel's Ethiopian policy. Egypt besieged the strait of Bab al-Mandab, and on 23 October 1973 Haile Selassie severed all diplomatic, as well as military and economic, relations with Israel.[11]

Non–Red Sea Arab States

Syria and Iraq

Since 1963, Syria has been under a Ba'thist, Pan-Arabist regime. Damascus is committed to Arab liberation throughout the Arab world and conceives Eritrea and the Eritreans as an integral part of that world. Despite Ethiopian nationalism and statehood and the ethnically and linguistically non-Arab background of the Eritreans, the 1952 constitution of the Ba'th Party defined the "Arab homeland" as "a national home for the Arabs. It consists of that area which extends beyond the Taurus Mountains . . . the Gulf of Basra, the Arabian Sea, the *Ethiopian mountains* [italics added] . . . the Atlantic Ocean and the Mediterranean Sea, and constitutes one single complete unit, and no part thereof may be alienated."[12] Syrian maps of the Arab world have always included Eritrea,[13] and the Syrian government has officially stated that "Syria's attitude is firm and clear. It supports the [Eritrean] revolution until the Eritrean people have full rights to self-determination, freedom, and independence."[14]

The Ba'th came to power in Syria at a most fortunate time from the Eritreans' point of view, for in the early 1960s President Nasser of Egypt had started ignoring their cause. According to Eritrean leaders, Syria proved to be a consistent supporter and provider.[15] In June 1963 (three months after the Ba'th had taken power), Idris Muhammad Adam opened the ELF office in Damascus,[16] and beginning in December 1965 Syrian radio enabled Uthman Sabi to broadcast frequently. Syrian arms were smuggled to the rebels, and—most important of all—Eritreans underwent yearlong training courses in the military academy at Aleppo.[17] (In 1968, for instance, some sixty Eritrean commanders reportedly received advanced training there.)

In July 1968 the Ba'th came to power in Iraq, and the Eritrean rebels became welcome guests in Baghdad. Following the split in the Eritrean movement, both Syria and Iraq (despite their mutual enmity) supported the same organization, the ELF-RC. As already mentioned, the main reason was that most Eritrean graduates of Syrian and Iraqi training schools belonged to this organization. (Indeed, when the younger generation took over the ELF-RC in the mid-1970s, Iraqi influence was to become an important factor in Eritrean affairs.) An Eritrean students' union affiliated with the ELF-RC was established in Baghdad. (The one affiliated with the EPLF had its head-quarters in Cairo.) Both Syria and Iraq consistently supported this organization with arms and training throughout the period under review (and continued to do so as of early 1982).[18]

The Palestine Liberation Organization

After the Six Day War, the Syrians could spare little for the Eritreans, and some of the Eritrean leaders began orienting their policy toward the emerging PLO. For their part, the Palestinians adopted the Ba'thist concept that the Eritreans were oppressed Arabs: "The Arabs have to understand," wrote a PLO journalist, "that [in Eritrea] a revolution in an Arab country is in the making, a revolution that is inseparable from the Arab liberation movement or from the struggle to liberate Palestine or from the Arab revolution in any other Arab country. We are therefore obliged to sympathize with the struggle of this people and support it in words and deeds."[19] Many Eritrean leaders (most notably, Uthman Sabi) expressed interest in making the Eritrean struggle "a main pillar of the Palestinian revolution."[20] Uthman Sabi revealed in May 1969 that Eritrean fighters had been receiving training in PLO camps.[21] Earlier in 1969, according to one source, a high-ranking PLO delegation led by Ali Hasan Salameh (later head of the Black September organization and architect of the 1972 massacre of Israeli athletes at the Munich Olympic Games) visited Eritrean guerrillas in the field.[22] As a result of his visit, the PLO undertook to train Eritrean fighters at its camps in Jordan, Lebanon, and Syria. According to another source, 250 Eritreans were undergoing training at PLO camps in Syria and Lebanon in early 1970.[23]

The key figure in the nurturing of these relations was Uthman Sabi. After his claims to leadership were rejected by the Syrian- and Iraqi-trained Eritrean field commanders in 1968, he found the PLO a good substitute for Baghdad and Damascus. It was in fact in a PLO base in Jordan that in November 1969 Uthman Sabi laid the first foundations of the EPLF.

PLO help in liberating "Arab Eritrea from Ethiopian occupation" and rescuing "the Arab Eritreans from the reactionary Ethiopian terror, which colludes with imperialism and cooperates with the Zionists," was most consistent.[24] Indeed, PLO training and support were major factors in shaping Eritrean tactics throughout this period; they were reflected in the sophisticated mining and ambushing, spectacular assassinations, and attempts at highjacking, which contributed significantly to the escalation of the conflict toward the end of 1970. As long as the Eritreans were active as guerrillas rather than as a conventional force, the PLO played an important role in improving their fighting ability.

Libya and South Yemen

The revolution that brought Col. Muammar al-Qadhdhafi to power in Libya in September 1969 brought the Eritrean movement an important and wealthy friend. As a Pan-Arabist, a dedicated supporter of Islamic solidarity, a fervent opponent of anything even remotely pro-Israel, and a self-nominated contender to Haile Selassie's position as an African leader, Qadhdhafi treated the Eritreans from the start as allies. (He may have had a special sympathy for the Eritreans because the Libyans had also been victims of Italian imperialism.) Qadhdhafi and Uthman Salih Sabi became closely associated, and in 1970 following the PLO defeat in Jordan and in 1971 following the anti-Eritrean change in Sudanese policy, Libya became the main source of finances and arms for the EPLF.[25]

The bulk of Libyan support was transferred to Eritrea through the PDRY, which was established in November 1967 and has been led ever since by the Arabist and radically Marxist National Liberation Front (NLF). The NLF allowed Uthman Sabi to operate from its Aden office, and many EPLF fighters received training in the neighboring town of Shayikh Uthman.[26] Although Ethiopian authorities warned the PDRY repeatedly that they would retaliate by acting against the Yemeni communities in Addis Ababa and other Ethiopian towns,[27] PDRY support for the EPLF continued throughout the period discussed.

The Red Sea Arab States

Egypt

Ethiopia and Egypt, two of the more ancient civilizations in the world, have for centuries enjoyed political, cultural, and religious relations. Eritrea has always played a pivotal role in this common history. The Egyptians controlled Massawa from 1848 and occupied most of present-day Eritrea from 1872 to 1884.[28] When conflict arose between Egypt and Ethiopia, Eritrea was the battleground on which it was resolved.[29] In the more recent past, Eritrea was again a pivotal issue in relations between the two states, with the Egyptians adopting an ambivalent attitude. In December 1950, for example, when the United Nations debated the future of Eritrea, Egypt voted for the establishment of the federation, ignoring the will of the Eritrean Muslims and condemnations by fellow Arabs.[30] Later, even when motivated by a strong sense of Pan-Arabism under Nasser's leadership, Egypt remained respectful of Ethiopian might and interests. The main reason was Ethiopia's central position in the "African circle," with which Nasser sought to identify. Another reason was the assumption that Ethiopia could cause Egypt heavy damage by constructing dams on the Blue Nile. Indeed, Nasser's special relations with Haile Selassie were a main feature of Egypt's African policy.

Yet Pan-Arabist Nasserite Egypt, affiliated also with the "Islamic circle," was not indifferent to the political aspirations of Muslims and Arabs in the Horn. Prior to the establishment of the independent Somali republic on 1 July 1960, Nasser was a strong supporter of Somali nationalism and remained a consistent supporter and supplier, even when Somalia began to make huge territorial claims with respect to Ethiopia and the two states became actively hostile. At the same time, President Nasser did his best to make Eritrean exiles feel at home in Egypt. During the 1950s, Walda-Ab Walda-Mariam was active in the Egyptian capital; and Eritrean students, mostly Muslims at al-Azhar University, were allowed to give free voice to their emotions. Later, with the split in the Eritrean movement, Cairo became the center of the Eritrean students' union affiliated with the EPLF. In 1958, a small training camp for Eritreans was opened near Alexandria, and some prominent commanders of the future received their first instruction there.[31]

Besides the rather insignificant support rendered directly to the separatists, Egypt was indirectly playing an important role in Eritrean affairs. Egypt's Pan-Arabist aspirations and regional activities constituted the greatest external threat to Ethiopia in the 1960s. The most relevant indication of this was the presence of an Egyptian army in neighboring Yemen from 1962 to 1967. It was clear at the time that the final objective of the Egyptians was not only to help republican Pan-Arabists gain power in remote Yemen, but also to obtain control of the Arabian Peninsula and the Red Sea basin. The pretext of supporting a local ally in order to deploy an invading army (which grew to some 70,000 men) was all too evident to Haile Selassie, and Ethiopia's annexation of Eritrea one month after the beginning of the Egyptian campaign in Yemen was no coincidence.

However, as long as the Egyptian army was fighting a losing battle in the mountains of Yemen, Addis Ababa and Cairo continued to conduct a policy of friendship. When the OAU was established in May 1963, the Ethiopian capital was chosen as its headquarters; and in early November of the same year, Haile Selassie, regarded by many as an African leader, paid an official visit to Egypt. "The talks between the two heads of state," according to

Egyptian radio, "took place in an atmosphere of fraternity, cordiality, and mutual understanding."[32] Nasser and Haile Selassie discussed regional affairs and totally ignored the question of Eritrean separatism. They "agreed on increased cooperation between the two countries in the political, economic, and cultural fields." (It was at this period that Eritrean separatists started pinning their hopes on Damascus.) In 1964, the training camp for Eritreans near Alexandria was transferred to Algeria.[33] In October 1966 Haile Selassie visited Nasser again and was again most cordially received.

However, Addis Ababa felt an indirect Egyptian threat. Cairo, entrenched in nearby Yemen, actively supported the Somalis in their conflict with Ethiopia over the Ogaden. In early 1967, Ethiopian fears of Egypt's regional plans increased. Britain announced in February that it would evacuate Aden within a year; Addis Ababa suspected that if the Egyptians, under Soviet auspices, captured Aden and South Yemen, Eritrea would become their next target. These fears were fanned by the renewal of anti-Ethiopian propaganda in the Egyptian media and by information that Egyptian agents and advisers frequently visited Eritrean rebel camps.[34] By late May 1967, amid growing Ethiopian suspicions, Ethiopia requested the Egyptian delegate of the Arab League in Addis Ababa, Qasim al-Hat, to leave the country.

Ethiopia greeted the Egyptian defeat in the Six Day War with deep satisfaction and relief. Israel's victory led to the Egyptian evacuation of Yemen by the end of the year. In retrospect, the Six Day War was a blow to Pan-Arabist aspirations in general and to Egyptian hegemony in particular. Historically it has almost always been the case that a militarily strong Egypt— in pharaonic times, under the Mameluks, Muhammad Ali, or Khedive Ismail—strove to obtain control over the Red Sea. Following its defeat, Egypt lost interest in the Red Sea (whose strategic importance diminished following the closure of the Suez Canal). Even in 1969, when revolutionary governments came to power in the Sudan, Libya, and Somalia and became active supporters of the Eritreans, Nasser's Egypt remained passive. In June 1970, Haile Selassie visited Nasser for the third time. (Nasser himself, though invited, always avoided visiting Ethiopia.) The purpose of the emperor's visit was to ask the president to restrain the Sudanese government, which was helping the Eritrean separatists. As a *quid pro quo*, Nasser demanded the expulsion of the Israelis from Ethiopia, and the matter was dropped.

With the coming to power of President Anwar Sadat following Nasser's death in September 1970, Egypt seemed to lose all interest in the Red Sea. In October 1972, for instance, Hasanayn Haikal, the opposition editor of *al-Ahram* and a devoted keeper of Nasser's legacy, lamented: "We, the Arabs, have to plan a new strategy that will guarantee full Arab sovereignty over the Red Sea. The integrity of the Red Sea was always a strategic line of Egypt during each of its periods of might, from the days of the great pharaohs till the

Arab republic of Gamal Abd al-Nasser. The Red Sea is an Arab Sea because all the coastal states that control it are Arab ones. These are Egypt, the Sudan, Saudi Arabia, North Yemen, and the PDRY."[35] But, he went on, certain changes were now jeopardizing all this: Egypt seemed to be turning its back to the Red Sea; the Sudan was wavering between various trends; Saudi Arabia had its own interests; North Yemen was busy with South Yemen and vice versa; and on top of it all, Ethiopia was active in the Red Sea and Israel still maintained a presence there.

The Sudan

Throughout history, Christian Ethiopia and the Islamic entities in the neighboring Sudan generally maintained a state of peaceful coexistence. Although occasionally interrupted by border disputes, raids, and counter-raids, and in the late 1880s even by an open war, the differences between them remained contained.[36] The Ethiopians refrained from invading the Sudan because they could not stand the hot, humid climate of the Nile basin; the Sudanese stayed out of Ethiopia because they could not tolerate the cold of mountainous Ethiopia. Even after the establishment of the Republic of Sudan in 1956, however, there was only one insignificant border dispute to mar the neighborly coexistence. Despite the lack of open conflict, both sides actively maintained indirect conflict by interfering in the other side's internal problems. The Sudanese involved themselves in Eritrea, and Ethiopia retaliated by supporting the Christian separatists in the southern Sudan (the Anya Nya movement), who started an open rebellion against the Khartoum government in September 1963. Aware, however, of Ethiopia's military superiority, the Sudanese refrained from pushing Ethiopia too far.

After the establishment of the federation in 1952, the Sudan became a natural center for exiles from neighboring Eritrea. The political leaders had their headquarters in Khartoum, and the military command at Kassala. Willingly or not, the Sudan was also the host country for the tens of thousands of refugees who fled Eritrea whenever the Ethiopian army accelerated its drive against Eritrean nationalism. Some of the refugees were recruited by the movement and trained in its camps. In early 1970, the number of Eritrean fighters in the Sudan was estimated at four hundred.[37] Moreover, Sudanese territory was the only land route for communication and supply to the Eritrean fighters in the field. The Ethiopian government therefore devoted its political skills and might to reaching an understanding with the Sudanese government. The mutuality of this understanding, as described by a Western observer in 1969, was that "Haile Selassie says little about the genocide in the Southern Sudan . . . the Sudan says little about the genocide in Eritrea."[38]

Throughout the period, however, there were fluctuations in this under-standing, and Sudanese support for the Eritreans varied accordingly. In October 1963, a month after the beginning of the rebellion in the southern Sudan, the Sudanese government, then under the military regime of Gen. Ibrahim Abud, extradited thirteen Eritrean fighters, who were later hanged in Addis Ababa.[39] In early 1964 the two governments discussed an extradition agreement.[40] If implemented, it would have constituted an insurmountable problem for the Eritrean separatists. By the end of the year, however, Ibrahim Abud's military government was toppled and a multiparty regime established in which leftists on the one hand and Muslim fundamentalists on the other advocated a pro-Eritrean policy. (In the religious wing of Sudanese politics, there was a strong element representing the Mighraniyya sect, which was centered on Kassala and had many adherents among Eritrean Bani Amirs.) In January 1965 the new Sudanese government brushed aside the draft of the extradition agreement,[41] and from then on the Eritrean separatists had a free run in Sudan and occasionally received direct, though not generous, support. In February 1967, Haile Selassie visited Khartoum and exchanged friendly declarations with President Ismail al-Azhari and Prime Minister Sadiq al-Mahdi.[42] In practice, however, the situation deteriorated, and on the eve of the Six Day War in the Middle East, both countries were concentrating forces along their common border.[43] The same pattern continued during 1968 and early 1969. While joint Ethiopian-Sudanese committees held discussions, Ethiopians were interfering in the southern Sudan and the Sudanese were interfering in Eritrea. (Following the split in the Eritrean movement, Sudanese aid was channeled to the ELF-RC.)

On 25 May 1969, a revolutionary regime under Col. Ja'far al-Numayri came to power in Khartoum. Sudan was declared a "people's republic," which was to follow a line of "Sudanese socialism." The new leadership strengthened the Sudanese commitment to Pan-Arabism and to liberation movements in Africa, and declarations by Sudanese officials aroused Eritrean expectations.[44] Immediately following Haile Selassie's visit to Khartoum in early 1970, Sudanese support for the separatists became visible and even massive by Eritrean standards.[45] Sudanese authorities enabled the Libyans, the Iraqis, the PLO, and others to send significant quantities of relatively new weapons to the area: assault rifles, heavy machine guns, mortars, bazookas, mines, explosives, and the like. This new Sudanese policy contributed directly to the 1970 escalation in Eritrea. Following the killing of Ergetu Tshome later that same year, Ethiopian officers pushed for retaliation against the Sudanese,[46] and some border clashes did take place. More significantly, the Ethiopians intensified their help to Christian separatists in the southern Sudan, enabling the Israelis to render support to the Anya Nya movement.[47]

Diplomats were then mobilized in an effort to ease the tension. In March 1971, the foreign ministers of the two countries signed a treaty in Khartoum prohibiting subversive activity. In June, the Sudanese foreign minister reciprocated by paying an official visit to Addis Ababa.

The next month, events in Khartoum led to the termination of Sudanese support for the separatists. Frustrated by Numayri's conciliatory policy vis-à-vis the Ethiopians, the Khartoum-based Eritreans ventured to interfere in Sudanese internal affairs. An abortive coup against Numayri engineered by Communists supported by Iraqi Ba'thists (who were then the main suppliers of the ELF General Command, the future ELF-RC) took place on 19–22 July. After the failure of the coup, Numayri was reportedly furious with the Eritreans involved. Their lives were spared only because of a personal request by Libya's Colonel Qadhdhafi, a great friend of Numayri's at the time. Subsequently their activities in Sudan were closely watched by local authorities, and they were prohibited from carrying arms on Sudanese soil.

In 1971 Numayri made constitutional and other changes necessary to solidify his power, including a far-reaching rapprochement with Haile Selassie. In November the Sudanese president spent six days in Addis Ababa, an invitation that he reciprocated by hosting the emperor in Khartoum during the first four days of 1972. On 28 February 1972, the two states signed a treaty recognizing each other's territorial integrity. In July 1972 another agreement settled the border dispute. Both parties agreed to avoid helping subversive movements in the other country.

On the whole, the so-called Addis Ababa Treaty was respected. As a direct result, Anya Nya leaders in the southern Sudan negotiated a political solution with Numayri, and Sudanese patrols sealed the Eritrean-Sudanese border.[48] Although communications between the guerrillas in the field and their fellows in Khartoum, and even the flow of some supplies to Eritrea, were not stopped entirely, the Ethiopian-Sudanese rapprochement was a great blow to the Eritrean movement, and until the 1974 revolution its ability to challenge the Ethiopian army was seriously diminished.

Somalia

Since its establishment in July 1960, the Republic of Somalia has been committed to the fulfillment of Somali ethnic nationalism and has claimed Somali-inhabited areas that Ethiopia occupied during the last quarter of the nineteenth century when it was struggling against European imperialism and which comprise nearly one-third of its territory. The Christian kingdom proved vital enough to expand and at the same time to increase its control over these regions through centralization. As a result, it managed not only to defeat the Italian invasion from Eritrea in 1896 but also to compete successfully with the Italians, the British, and the French for control of Somali-populated areas. For the Somalis, the Ethiopian occupation was as imperialistic and colonialist as any other, and they were vocal in their support for the Eritreans.

In practical terms, the Somali contribution was nearly meaningless, but the Somalis were very active verbal supporters. In June 1963, Idris Adam opened an office in Mogadishu.[49] During the first years of the Eritrean struggle, Somali radio was the chief carrier of the separatists' voice. Its frequent broadcasts of ELF-supplied information from the field strongly denounced "savage Abyssinia" as a Christian country under "a stone-age, savage, feudalist rule" that oppressed Muslims.[50] Occasionally, following Somali tradition, political poems were broadcast: one of them, in May 1963, proved twelve years later to be a true prophecy of the personal fate of Ethiopia's emperor: "Haile Selassie has blinded the Eritreans and erased their name from the map . . . The time has come when all will unite against him. He will be killed and his body thrown into an unknown place."[51]

In the meantime, however, Haile Selassie was alive and well, and his country was militarily far superior to Somalia. In 1964, Somali provocations ended with a humiliating defeat of the Somali army at the hands of Aman Andom. In October of the following year, the two countries signed an agreement to cease hostile propaganda. Although propaganda warfare was later resumed, the Eritrean issue virtually ceased to figure in Somali media.

The coming to power in October 1969 of Siad Barre's socialist military regime brought no significant change. The Somalis desisted from any action, patiently awaiting the death of Haile Selassie. (To avoid further provocations, President Siad cut off the support Somalia had long been giving to rebels in the Ethiopian province of Bale. Consequently the revolt of the local Oromos collapsed in 1970.) In the meantime the Somalis modernized and enlarged their armed forces with generous Soviet aid and supervised the establishment and growth of the Western Somali Liberation Front (WSLF) in Ethiopia. In February 1974 they joined the Arab League.

Saudi Arabia

Until the late 1960s, Saudi Arabia was a kingdom on the defensive in the Red Sea arena. Rich enough to attract the eyes of hungry neighbors, it was not yet strong enough to deter them from challenging its very existence. The main threat was presented by Nasserite Egypt, which used a combination of Pan-Arabism and a massive military presence in neighboring Yemen to undermine the Saudi regime. The Saudis therefore could not afford to support the Eritreans beyond token donations and occasional media accusations that Ethiopia was oppressing Muslims.[52] Whatever their interest in Ethiopia's religious affairs, however, the Saudis were more suspicious of the Eritreans' leftist and increasingly Marxist revolutionary image. For obvious reasons, this was truer after the establishment of the EPLF. Uthman Salih Sabi was trying his best to befriend Saudi princes and emphasize Eritrea's Arabism, but he could not conceal from the Saudis that the majority of EPLF fighters were Christians and leftists.

Thus, although the Saudis took the political initiative in the Persian Gulf and the Arabian Peninsula following the decline of Nasserism in the early 1970s, they were reluctant to conduct an active Red Sea policy. The potential local Islamic and Arab allies, the Eritreans and the Somalis, were leftists. From the Saudi point of view, it was safer if both were restrained by the might of conservative, pro-Western Ethiopia. Even when Saudi Arabia emerged as a state of great regional influence and power after the Yom Kippur War in 1973, it refrained from interfering in the neighboring Horn of Africa. As long as Haile Selassie was in power, the Saudis supported the status quo in the Red Sea. In January 1974, Haile Selassie received a warm welcome in Riyadh from King Faisal, and the richest king alive gave famine-striken Ethiopia a token $35 million as a reward for its recent breaking of relations with Israel.[53]

After the Ethiopian Revolution

The 1974 revolution in Ethiopia also marked a turning point in the attitude of neighboring Arab states. They now began to conceive the Red Sea as a cohesive strategic system. This new concept developed gradually. The first stage involved a change of attitude toward support for the Eritrean separatists. When the Suez Canal reopened in 1975, the Red Sea once again became one of the most important waterways in the world. Then, as a reaction to the ensuing Ethiopian alliance with the Soviet Union in 1977, Saudi Arabia, Egypt, and the Sudan began to coordinate policy under the slogan of "Arabization of the Red Sea." The implications of this new reality for the Eritrean conflict from 1975 on are dealt with below. It is, however, important to observe here that the first stage in this fundamental change—namely, the adoption of a pro-Eritrean policy by the neighboring Arabs (primarily the Saudis)—contributed greatly to the outbreak of the open war in Eritrea in early 1975.

It was, no doubt, a major achievement for the Eritrean movement. However, despite the common opinion that the Eritrean problem was a result of Arab interference in Ethiopian affairs, events tell a different story. Muhammad Said, director of information of the EPLF, said in an interview in April 1975: "We are not being pushed by the Arabs. When we started our struggle fourteen years ago, we were not even allowed to move freely in the Arab countries. Our struggle began a long time ago inside Eritrea, and we only received arms from the Arabs four years ago."[54] Although Eritrean leaders tried persistently before 1974 to build an "Arab bridge" over the Red Sea, those Arab states whose support could have been meaningful did not respond enthusiastically.

The moving spirit in the effort to create this bridge was Uthman Salih Sabi. He conceived Eritrean nationalism in a Pan-Arabist context, sparing no effort to emphasize the strategic importance of Eritrea to the overall struggle of the Arabs. In 1969, for example, he stated in an interview given to an Arab newspaper that "the imperialist factors in the Red Sea are the imperialist Zionists . . . Their aim is to exploit the Eritrean coast against the Arab nation and the Arab revolution . . . but the Eritrean revolution is on guard and is the guarantee that this will be corrected, until finally the Red Sea will become a purely Arab Sea."[55] This view did not reflect a consensus in the Eritrean movement concerning Eritrea's Arabism.[56] Its frequent expression at the time, however, indicates the Eritreans' interest in eliciting Arab support.[57] In October 1974, for example, Eritrean representatives at the Rabat Conference of the Arab League submitted a request to join the League's committees as observers "and thus make it possible for the Arab people of Eritrea, who are an integral part of the Arab nation . . . to become a member of the Arab League upon gaining independence."[58]

But as long as Ethiopia was strong, the Red Sea Arab states preferred to ignore the Eritrean call. It took the Ethiopian revolution, which destroyed the machinery of state and rendered the country militarily weak and diplomatically isolated, to activate the interest of these states in helping to create an Arab state in Eritrea.

Another relevant factor was the ideological change in Addis Ababa—the establishment of the Derg and the adoption of leftist and revolutionary doctrines after late 1974. The radicalization of the Ethiopian regime created a new reality for the Saudis, as well as for the Egyptians and the Sudanese. The Eritrean problem was now seen as a conflict between a revolutionary, increasingly Marxist Ethiopian regime and a movement led by (or so it seemed, due to Uthman's efforts) advocates of Arabism and Islamic solidarity.

The policy adopted by the Derg in November 1974 of seeking a military solution in Eritrea was also an important factor in the making of this process. Before the killing of Aman Andom, when a political solution was sought in the province, Ethiopia enjoyed good relations with some of its Red Sea neighbors. In Egypt, where Aman's brother was Ethiopia's ambassador, the Ethiopian revolution was conceived as a great victory for the Arab cause. In September 1974 an Egyptian analyst even suggested that "there is no room whatsoever for hesitation; we have to support the Ethiopian regime, for such support is direct aid to an ally in the context of the Arab struggle in general and the battle for the liberation of the occupied territories in Palestine in particular . . . Good relations between Ethiopia and the Arabs may well result in the closure of the

[Eritrean] ports of Massawa and Assab to Israeli ships, and thus the Red Sea, from the gates of the Indian Ocean to its northern edge, will become a purely Arab sea.[59]

Sudanese President Numayri appreciated Aman's (and Zawde Gabra-Sellase's) efforts to solve the Eritrean problem politically and offered his services as a mediator. The Somalis, for their part, expressed their approval of this approach in surprisingly warm words.[60]

But even prior to the killing of Aman and the failure of his policy, the Red Sea Arab states started supporting the Eritreans. As early as June 1974 Uthman Salih Sabi met with King Faisal of Saudi Arabia, who, though reportedly uneasy about the radicalism of EPLF, promised his aid. In September Uthman again met with the Saudi king and was promised generous financial and diplomatic support. Following this meeting, the Saudi foreign minister conducted talks with his Sudanese colleague, and in December both Saudi Arabia and Sudan started supplying or authorizing the transfer of arms to the separatists.[61] Reports in October 1974 and February 1975 indicated that Egypt had joined them.[62] In February 1975, the rich Kuwaitis expressed their strong solidarity with Eritrea, "a dear part of the Arab nation."[63] The only improvement from the Ethiopian point of view was made by Libya. Qadh-dhafi, Haile Selassie's sworn enemy, established diplomatic relations with Ethiopia two weeks after the emperor's deposition.[64] He continued to finance the separatists, however, and thus did not fully betray his friend Uthman Sabi.[65]

Thus, one year after the 1974 revolution—despite Ethiopia's breaking of relations with Israel and its intensive diplomatic effort to appease the Arabs[66]—it faced an unprecedented Arab challenge to its territorial integrity. The Eritrean movement, however, was growing stronger and mobilizing thousands of young Eritreans. The local rebellion was rapidly becoming an open war within a regional context.

6. Eritrean Victories, 1975–1977

The agreement between the EPLF and the ELF-RC at Koazien on 31 January 1975 initiated a new period in the Eritrean conflict. Until then, the Eritreans had confined themselves to classic guerrilla warfare. They gained control over parts of the countryside, ambushed army convoys, and performed occasional assassinations and acts of terrorism in the main towns. Their general military concept was summarized in 1969 by Uthman Sabi: "We are not ready for an offensive to drive the Ethiopians out of the cities. That time may not come until the death of Haile Selassie, when we anticipate Ethiopia will probably fall apart."[1]

Now the time was apparently ripe for change. The night following the Koazien agreement, hundreds of guerrillas slipped into Asmara itself; this was the beginning of the February Battle, the first major engagement of the Eritrean war in an urban center. The battle lasted three weeks, with hundreds of casualties on both sides.[2] The Eritreans failed to take the town, however, and their exercise in massive urban terrorism did not seriously challenge Ethiopian control of Asmara. Bleeding heavily, they had to withdraw. At the end of February, a combined EPLF–ELF-RC effort to capture Keren also failed.[3] Yet February 1975 marked a turning point; from then on, the Eritreans took the military initiative. In an attempt to defeat the Ethiopian army in its own camps and to occupy urban centers, they switched to conventional warfare and gradually but surely gained ground.

Several reasons led to this change. First, there was a profound quantitative revolution in the separatist forces. Before mid-1974, the number of active fighters in both organizations was estimated at between 2,000 and 2,500,[4] but the failure of Aman Andom's policy, the weakness and increasing brutality of the Ethiopian army, and the financial and political support rendered to the separatists by their powerful Arab neighbors persuaded many younger Eritreans to leave the urban and rural centers and join the rebel camp. In early 1975, the number of insurgents was variously estimated at 6,000, 6,000–15,000, and even 26,000.[5] By the middle of 1976, estimates ran higher, reaching 20,000, 25,000, and even 30,000–45,000.[6] By early 1977, estimates ranged from 38,500 to 43,000.[7] (These figures were most probably inflated by Eritrean propagandists and undoubtedly included barely trained militia forces as well as front-line fighters.)

Second, the Ethiopian army's ability to fight was greatly diminished as a result of the revolution. The 2d Division, like the rest of the Ethiopian army, was politicized, and this directly affected discipline and fighting morale. (As discussed below, this phenomenon influenced developments in Addis Ababa, too.) Quantitatively as well, the Ethiopian army could hardly cope with the new reality in the province. Even with reinforcements from the 1st Division, the territorial army, and other units, the number of Ethiopian soldiers in Eritrea between 1975 and 1977 did not exceed 25,000.[8] As the separatist forces grew, Ethiopia could not maintain all its military positions in Eritrea. In early 1975, the army began to evacuate most company-size camps and garrisons and reorganize them in urban centers where at least a battalion could be maintained. According to one source, in early 1976 the Ethiopian army garrisoned only 17 of the 60 towns and rural centers it had previously held.[9] The evacuation left most of western Eritrea under the separatists' control. The effect was such that without scoring a victory, the rebels could organize freely and launch offensives whenever they pleased from the middle of 1975 on.[10]

Third, the EPLF and ELF-RC were undergoing an important qualitative change. Most of the new recruits were members either of the urban intelligentsia—secondary-school graduates, university students, and the like—or former policemen and commandos, and the majority were Christian Tigreans. It is estimated that by mid-1976 Christians constituted half of the separatist forces.[11] These factors contributed to profound ideological, organizational, and political changes in both organizations. Militarily, it had a double effect: it greatly improved the organizations' ability to adopt sophisticated weaponry, and the new recruits (unlike the tribal nomads) persistently endeavored to return to their native towns as liberators.

Fourth, in late 1974, the Eritreans' financial resources increased, and they acquired new types of arms. This supply would later diminish due to a growing split between the field commanders and the Arab-based exiles, but in the meantime, such leaders as Uthman Sabi and Idris Adam channeled weapons and money to their respective organizations: from Libya, the PDRY, and Saudi Arabia to the EPLF, and from Iraq, the Sudan, and Syria to the ELF-RC.

Fifth, although the military cooperation agreed to at Koazien was maintained only occasionally and failed to lead to political rapprochement, it was nevertheless meaningful. According to the EPLF, in 1975, fifteen battles were conducted in cooperation with ELF-RC units.[12]

Sixth, the whole strategic situation in northern Ethiopia changed after the 1974 revolution. Revolts and unrest in the provinces of Bagemdir, Tigre, and in the Afar-populated areas of southern Eritrea and eastern Wallo created a buffer zone between Eritrea and Addis Ababa. This area was fertile soil for the establishment of several political and military organizations, which cooperated with the Eritrean separatists because they were opposed to the Derg.

The *Ethiopian Democratic Union* (EDU) was established in early 1975 by three prominent members of the prerevolutionary Ethiopian establishment who were not personally identified with Haile Selassie's regime. Lieutenant General Iyasu Mangasha, army chief of staff in the late 1950s and early 1960s and then ambassador to London until the revolution, was a Christian Tigrean with Eritrean affiliations. *Ras* Mangasha Siyum, a great-grandson of (the Tigrean) Emperor Yohannes IV, had been governor of Tigre since 1961 and was a strong opponent of Haile Selassie's policy of Amharization. In October 1974 he escaped imprisonment by the Derg and fled to the Sudan, from where he made sporadic visits to Tigre and Bagemdir to organize his followers. Lieutenant General Naga Tagene was a native of Bagemdir, a former commander of the 3rd Division, and a close associate of Aman Andom. Under their leadership, the EDU's objective was to replace the Derg with a democratic, liberal government.[13] The EDU was not an important factor in the capital, but it reflected local resistance to the new regime in the provinces of Tigre and Bagemdir. The EDU enjoyed the active support of Saudi Arabia and the Sudan and cooperated from the start with the Eritreans, although as Ethiopian nationalists their ideology prevented them from supporting Eritrean separatism. They favored "a federal system for Ethiopia" in which "the right of the Eritrean people to determine democratically their own destiny, coupled with the according of proper weight to interests of the rest of Ethiopia," would be implemented.[14] Although some military cooperation was achieved between the EDU and the Eritreans (the ELF-RC),[15] the EDU's greatest contribution to the Eritrean cause was indirect: its struggle with the Ethiopian army over control of Bagemdir and western Tigre from 1975 to 1977 turned one of the two main highways from central Ethiopia to Eritrea into a via dolorosa for the Ethiopian army. The EDU's activities peaked in early 1977 when it nearly captured the town of Metemma, held Humera and Dabat, and temporarily blocked the main road to Gondar.

The *Tigrean People's Liberation Front* (TPLF) was formed by young natives of Tigre province who wanted to exploit the revolution in order to advance Tigrean nationalism and were unwilling, as leftists, to identify with *Ras* Mangasha and the EDU. The organization was established in late 1974 under collective leadership, and it gained fame by kidnapping British journalists.[16] Throughout late 1975 and 1976, it managed to maintain control over some parts of Tigre and to create difficulties for the Ethiopian army on the main highway from Addis Ababa to Asmara. However, as in the case of the EDU, identifying with the goals of the Eritreans was problematic for the TPLF. Tigrean nationalism encompasses, by definition, all Tigreans residing in Eritrea, making Eritreanism and Tigreanism seem incompatible.

Yet, in practice, both movements had much to gain by a common struggle against Addis Ababa. Indeed, in the past, Asmara—as a political center independent of Addis Ababa under the Italians and the British—had always supported Tigreanism for strategic reasons. It was therefore natural that the TPLF cooperated extensively with the EPLF.[17] It gave actual military support to the Eritreans in two instances: in Tigre itself, it helped to wipe out the Ethiopian-trained militia in May 1976 (the so-called Peasants March, described below), which was preparing to launch an attack on the Eritreans. Then, in early 1977 it captured many rural centers in Tigre, as well as the town of Abbi Addi. In the short periods it maintained control, the TPLF temporarily expanded the buffer zone between Eritrea and Ethiopia.

The *Ethiopian People's Revolutionary Army* (EPRA) was the military wing of the Ethiopian People's Revolutionary Party (EPRP), a movement opposed to the Derg and centered in Addis Ababa. Both were established in the second half of 1975 and recognized the Eritreans' right to self-determination. The military wing became quite active in cooperating with the EPLF (but not the TPLF) in fighting the Ethiopian army in Tigre. In 1977 its forces in Tigre were estimated at five hundred fighters.

The *Afar Liberation Front* (ALF) aimed to fulfill Afar ethnic and linguistic nationalism, but even though not directly concerned with the territorial nationalism of Eritrea, it cooperated with the separatists (ELF-RC only).[18] Established in March 1975, the ALF was led by Hanfari Ali Mira, the son of the Afars' traditional leader, Sultan Ali Mira, who had left Ethiopia for Saudi Arabia after the Derg's proclamation of land reform in March 1975. His son's organization was supplied by the Saudis (as was the EDU, with which the ALF was closely associated). The ALF's main contribution to the Eritrean struggle was to create difficulties for the Ethiopians on the strategic road from the Eritrean port of Assab to Addis Ababa.

These factors contributed to the Eritreans' growing confidence in a military victory. Throughout 1975 and 1976, hundreds of small battles and clashes took place. In the overwhelming majority, the Eritreans were the initiators and often the victors.[19] Both sides, as well as noncombatants, paid dearly in blood. One estimate put the number of military and civilian casualties in the first third of 1975 at about 10,000; the EPLF estimated the number of dead civilians at the end of the same year at 25,000.[19] The Ethiopian army could do little to retaliate other than to initiate occasional punitive ground attacks or aerial bombardments of villages held by rebel organizations.[20] According to the EPLF, Ethiopian forces destroyed some 110 Eritrean villages in 1975 alone.[21] Such acts, combined with a campaign to cut food supplies to drought-stricken areas in the hands of the rebels, served only to further alienate the Eritreans.[22] Confident that time was on their side, the Eritrean organizations categorically refused even to consider the peace plan offered on 16 May 1976 by the Derg (see Chapter 9). Other efforts at mediation, such as President Numayri's, met with the firm demand that any discussion concerning the future of Eritrea be conducted on the basis of Eritrean self-determination.

From a military point of view, the Ethiopians could do nothing in Eritrea before building a new and stronger army. The 25,000 troops stationed in the province constituted no less than half their armed forces. Even so, they were bleeding heavily.[23] The rest of the army was busy maintaining the regime while facing growing opposition in almost every province. It was also preparing to meet a Somali challenge in the Ogaden, or perhaps Djibouti. A new division, named the Flame (Nebalbal), started training in early 1975 (under Israeli instructors, now invited back by the new regime). The building and training of what was planned to be an elite corps was a lengthy procedure, and when some of the division's battalions were deployed in Eritrea in late 1976, they made little impact on the war.[24] The military solution, from the Ethiopian point of view, could not wait until the building, supplying, and training of a new and full-size professional army.

The first Ethiopian attempt to respond to the growing challenge in Eritrea was the so-called Peasants March. On 2 March 1976, 84 local leaders from the northern provinces of Tigre, Bagemdir, Wallo, and Gojjam assembled in Addis Ababa. The head of the state, Brig. Gen. Tafari Banti, briefed them on the situation in Eritrea and called on them to help organize a crusade against the Muslims invading the province.[25] A militia numbering some 200,000 or more armed and trained members of the newly organized peasants' associations would march to Eritrea and crush the rebels by sheer numerical superiority. At the same time, the very organization of the militia in the northern provinces would help buttress the revolution there. For the next few months, under the direction of Lt. Col. Atnafu Abate, the second vice-chairman of the Derg, northern Ethiopia saw what had not been seen in Ethiopia since Haile Selassie started building a Western-trained army in the early 1940s: tens of thousands of peasants undergoing military training clad in traditional white *shammas* and armed with ancient British, Belgian, and Italian rifles (for which the Derg sent ammunition-purchasing missions to Turkey, Yugoslavia, and Italy).[26] No revolutionary phraseology was used. Derg members and priests told the peasants that they were defending Mother Ethiopia—crusaders facing a Muslim jihad. Once they had liberated Eritrea, the land would be distributed among them.[27]

The organization of the Peasants March symbolized the profound change in Eritrea. Till then, the Ethiopians had claimed that their army was dealing with gangs of *shifta*. Now the situation seemed to be quite the opposite; the Eritrean organizations were rapidly becoming regular armies, while the Ethiopians were about to launch a "beggars' crusade." Ethiopia gained little. At the end of May, the peasants, some 30,000–40,000 in number, were attacked in their camps by TPLF, ELF-RC, and EPLF units; those elements of the peasants' militia who managed to enter Eritrea (in Akalla-Guzai, near Um Hager, and in the Afars' region) were slain or imprisoned during early June.[28]

The Peasants March met with the strong disapproval of the United States, still the main supplier of arms to the Ethiopian army. This was partly because, as an exotic phenomenon, preparations for the campaign had gained worldwide publicity; it was referred to as a "barbaric march" and a plan for mass murder in Eritrea. (Although, as we have seen, it only remained to be seen who was about to be slain.)[29]

The news about preparations for the campaign, combined at the time with other revelations concerning violations of human rights in Addis Ababa, worsened the already deteriorating relations between the Derg and the United States. On 13 June 1976, the campaign was officially canceled.[30]

A failure in itself, the Peasants March served as a lesson for some policymakers in the Derg. In the future, peasant militias would be recruited mainly from the southern provinces and would be intensively trained and equipped with modern weapons by someone other than the United States. Within two years this combination of massive mobilization of peasants loyal to the revolution and massive Soviet arms supply would create a new military balance in the Horn.

In the meantime, the Eritrean separatists were clearly the victors. Following the failure of the Peasants March, the Ethiopian garrisons were demoralized.[31] The Sudan became an active supplier and supporter of the ELF-RC, EDU, and others. By the beginning of the rainy season in July 1976, the Eritreans had placed practically all the Ethiopian garrisons in Eritrea under active siege. The EPLF's share in the fighting was bigger than the ELF-RC's, for in western Eritrea the Ethiopians remained entrenched only in Sabdrat, Agordat, Tessenei, and Barentu. Keren, which lay in a region controlled by both organizations, was assaulted in October 1976 by a combined EPLF–ELF-RC force, but the old fort that *Ras* Alula had found invincible when he tried to oust the Egyptians in 1879 and had frustrated the British for weeks in 1941 would not fall. On 5 January 1977, Karora became the first Eritrean town to be captured by the EPLF.[32] On 23 March 1977, the ELPF captured its first district capital, Naqfa in the Sahil. The town had been surrounded since June 1976, and Ethiopian efforts to raise the siege had been frustrated.[33] By the time Naqfa fell, the ELF-RC had captured Um Hager, and on 22 April 1977 it took Tessenei. The Ethiopian garrison at Barentu continued to hold out even though it had been deprived of its airfield.[34] Then on 8 July 1977, only two days after the EPLF took Decamere, it captured Keren—the key to control of western and northern Eritrea—after a long, fierce battle that claimed the lives of some 2,000 Ethiopian soldiers, and in which 2,500 others were taken prisoner.[35] During the first week of August, the EPLF captured Digsa and the ELF-RC Saganaiti, and Asmara was put under full siege. By the end of September 1977, only Asmara, Massawa, Ginda, Dongolo, Barentu, Addi Qaih, and far-off Assab remained in Ethiopian hands.

By that time, Ethiopia had already built substantial new forces and was training more. A new Soviet-supplied and Cuban-trained army of some 250,000 men in regular and militia units was in the making. The political implications of this process are dealt with in Chapter 9. Militarily, the new army's main priority was fighting the Eritreans.[36] Throughout May and June 1977, the new forces deployed in the north managed to destroy the EDU and the TPLF, eliminating the buffer zone.[37] Then, in August, the first attempt to start a counteroffensive in Eritrea itself began. It had to be halted, however, because of the 23 July Somali invasion of Ethiopia. The surprised Ethiopians had to postpone the Eritrean campaign and concentrate on matters in the south. In the battle for the Ogaden, the Somalis exploited their superiority in armor and swept the desert. By September they had occupied it all, including the strategic town of Jijiga. Yet, they were unable to capture Harar and Dire-Dawa, and the springboard from the Ethiopian heights to the desert remained in Ethiopian hands. Soviet advisers and Cuban fighters were actively involved in helping, even rescuing, the Ethiopians. In early November, Somalia broke relations with the Soviet Union. The Soviets increased their support to Ethiopia (Cuban units led the field), and in the first week of March 1978, the defeated Somali army returned to its border.

The Ogaden War was a most important event in the history of the Horn of Africa and the Red Sea, with significant implications for U.S.-Soviet relations. From the Eritrean point of view, however, it signified the culmination of a regional process that had created conditions favorable for the fulfillment of Eritrean nationalism. In late 1977, the Eritreans seemed to have everything on their side. They controlled most of Eritrea, and Ethiopia was preoccupied with the Somalis. More important, they now had well-organized, highly motivated, battle-experienced, well-supplied armies capable of liberating the whole province. Finally, 1977 had seen the emergence of an Arab desire to Arabize the Red Sea. Saudi Arabia, Egypt, and the Sudan were interested in the establishment of an Arab Eritrea. In late 1977 it seemed to many that nothing could stop the Eritreans from fulfilling their ambitions—nothing except their own disunity, jealousies, and ideological dogmatism.

7. "Arabization of the Red Sea," 1975–1977

From the outset, the main objective of Eritrean leaders in the sphere of foreign relations was to create united Arab interest in their victory, but this did not materialize until after the revolution in Ethiopia. Far-off Ba'thist Syria and Iraq, the PLO, the PDRY, and Libya all responded warmly to the Eritreans' call, but their aid could not be decisive. The switch from subversive activities to the kind of war that would lead to the liberation of towns and an independent state would require the active help of the neighboring Arab states—Saudi Arabia, the Sudan, and Egypt.

But these states were too respectful of Haile Selassie's military and political might to support the Eritreans openly; the Eritreans emphasized their Arabism to little avail. As the Eritreans succeeded in their military endeavors and began to defeat the outnumbered and demoralized Ethiopian army, however, the Red Sea Arabs became interested in the establishment of an Arab Eritrea for their own reasons. The combination of Eritrean military superiority with the simultaneous emergence of a pro-Eritrean Arab consensus led by its rich and influential neighbor, Saudi Arabia, seemed at the time to promise prompt fulfillment of Eritrean nationalist aspirations.

As a result of what seemed to be the dismemberment of Ethiopia following the revolution and the emergence of a leftist-oriented regime in Addis Ababa, Saudi Arabia, the Sudan, Kuwait, and Egypt started in late 1974 to support the Eritrean separatists. By that time, an Arab concept of the Red Sea as a cohesive strategic arena was already in the making. During the Yom Kippur War, Egypt had closed the Bab al-Mandab strait to Israeli oil tankers going from Iran to Elat. In late October 1974 at the Rabat Conference, the Arab summit agreed to lease the island of Perim, located in the middle of the strait, from the PDRY for 99 years in order to secure "Arab" (namely, Saudi-Egyptian) control over the southern part of the Red Sea.[1]

Following the reopening of the Suez Canal in June 1975, the Red Sea became one of the most important waterways of the globe. After eight years, oil was again being shipped from the Persian Gulf to the West through the Red Sea. This time, however, the black gold was dearer by far and far more strategically important to Europe and the United States. After years of neglecting their interests in the Red Sea, the Western powers now found the Soviet Union well entrenched along its coasts. The PDRY was a Soviet ally, as was Somalia.

Soviet influence in Somalia, which started long before Siad Barre came to power on 21 October 1969, had by 1972 turned into full penetration. In return for arming the 17,000-man Somali army, the Soviets gained bases at Mogadishu and Kismayu and a most important naval base at Berbera. Soviet strategists attributed great importance to the Indian Ocean and the Red Sea. They were probably motivated by the dual aim of securing port facilities and bases for the growing Soviet navy and of securing the alliance of anti-Western regimes along this vital artery of the Western economy. In July 1974 the Soviet-Somali alliance was sealed by an official treaty. In 1975, when the canal was reopened, Ethiopia, too, seemed about to be lost to the West, as the Derg (though still aided by the United States and Israel) inclined more and more toward Marxism.

It was against this background of Soviet penetration that—with the indirect backing of the United States—Saudi Arabia, the Sudan, and Egypt raised such slogans as: "The Red Sea Is a Sea of Peace"; "No Superpower Involvement in the Red Sea"; and "The Red Sea Is an Arab Sea."

Thus, Hasanayn Haikal's 1972 call to build an all-Arab Red Sea policy was actualized during 1976—but now, this plan was aimed less at Israel than at the Soviets. The practical policy of the Riyadh-Khartoum-Cairo axis in the Red Sea was to fight Soviet encroachment and undermine existing Soviet positions through the use of Saudi money, Sudanese diplomacy, and Egyptian influence. The Saudis were the most experienced and the most influential in this context. In the late 1960s and early 1970s, they had proved their ability to face Soviet influence in Yemen and the Persian Gulf and were willing to invest heavily in luring the Somalis away from their Soviet allies. Throughout 1975 and 1976, the more the Derg resorted to Marxist phraseology, the more the Saudis rendered aid to its rivals. The EDU, the ALF, and other organizations received money and arms. Saudi aid was channeled to the Eritreans through Uthman Salih Sabi beginning in 1974. In Saudi and Saudi-financed media, the

Eritrean struggle was once again portrayed as a fight by Muslims against non-Muslim oppression.[2]

The Sudanese had to be more cautious with Ethiopia than the Saudis did. President Numayri was reportedly furious with the Derg following the killing of Aman Andom, whose Eritrean policy he had supported. Yet Sudanese aid to the separatists had to be cut back in mid-1975 because of renewed troubles in the southern Sudan. During May and June of that year, some six thousand refugees from the southern Sudan crossed into Ethiopia,[3] thus giving Ethiopia a strong card against Numayri. When, on 9 May 1976, the Derg published a nine-point plan for a political solution in Eritrea on the basis of self-administration, Numayri urged the Eritreans to accept it. He offered his services as mediator and was praised by a prominent associate of Colonel Mangistu.

However, an undercurrent of mutual suspicion between these neighboring states continued to characterize their relationship. The Derg had clearly adopted a Marxist line and in organizing the Peasants March had demonstrated that given the opportunity, it would again seek a military solution in Eritrea. Furthermore, there was clear evidence that Mangistu was persistently strengthening his relations with Colonel Qadhdhafi of Libya, now the sworn enemy of both Numayri of Sudan and Sadat of Egypt.

In July 1976, Numayri barely survived an attempted coup by a former prime minister, supposedly financed by Qadhdhafi and aided by Mangistu. During the trials that followed, 96 of the conspirators were accused of undergoing training in Ethiopian camps. Sudanese-Ethiopian relations, which since early 1972 had been correct, now became openly hostile. On 27 December 1976, Numayri announced that camps for the concentration of various forces opposed to his regime were being built in Ethiopia with the help of Libya and communist countries, and he warned of the possibility of an armed invasion.[4] The Sudanese president gave notice that what he called Ethiopia's plotting against his country would lead the Sudan to utilize the thousands of Eritrean refugees to cause unrest in Ethiopia. In early 1977, the Sudan and Ethiopia recalled their ambassadors and exchanged threats of armed invasion.[5] At the end of January, the Sudan announced its open support for the Eritrean movement and began extending aid to the EDU, the ELF-RC, and a new Eritrean organization, the ELF-PLF. At the same time, Numayri urged the United Nations to recognize "the just struggle of the oppressed Eritreans."[6] In May he expressed his warm support for the Eritrean nationalists, who were then, as he put it, "going from strength to strength capturing Eritrean towns in the fight for the liberation of their country from a foreign invader."[7]

The deterioration in Sudanese-Ethiopian relations led to Egypt's involvement in the Horn. After the attempted coup against Numayri in July 1976,

Sudan and Egypt signed a mutual defense agreement. Both were suspicious of Soviet encroachment and concerned about Libyan plots against their regimes. In early 1977, as Sudanese-Ethiopian tension was building, President Sadat declared that he would come to the support of Sudan in the event of open Sudanese-Ethiopian hostilities, and the defense ministers of both countries signed an official declaration to this effect.[8] At the same time, Egypt began to give low-profile support to the Eritreans.[9]

By mid-1976 Saudi Arabia, the Sudan, and Egypt—all suspicious of the Soviet presence in the area—coordinated their policies and called for the Arabization of the Red Sea. In July Saudi Arabia joined the Egyptian-Sudanese committee on military coordination,[10] and in November Saudi Arabia's King Khalid paid a visit to Khartoum, where he reportedly discussed with Numayri matters relating to Sudanese-Saudi-Egyptian strategic cooperation in the Red Sea, including Saudi plans to secure a strong naval presence there.[11] Under Saudi auspices, the Sudan became the pivotal factor in the making of an Arab Red Sea policy in the African coast. Sudanese-Somali relations improved significantly,[12] and in November 1976 a Sudanese military delegation visited Baghdad and Damascus, apparently to discuss the transfer of arms from Iraq and Syria to the Eritreans.[13] On 18 January 1977, a Kuwaiti newspaper reported that a Saudi-Sudanese-Egyptian body with the aim of coordinating the defense of the Red Sea had been established, and that Yemen and Jordan, together with Djibouti and Eritrea once they achieved independence, would be expected to join it.[14]

On 28 February 1977, the presidents of Egypt, Syria, and the Sudan met in Khartoum, issued a joint declaration that the subject of stability and peace in the Red Sea had become a matter of top priority for Arabs, and alleged that Ethiopia and Israel were contemplating moves against peace in this area. Following the meeting, President Asad of Syria told journalists that the three leaders had concluded that the Red Sea was an Arab sea and that Ethiopia had lost its foothold there because of the success of the Eritrean struggle supported by the Sudan, Saudi Arabia, and North Yemen.[15]

With the Saudis supporting him, Numayri redoubled his efforts to coordinate Arab Red Sea policy. At the end of March 1977, he participated in a mini-summit in Ta'izz in North Yemen, attended also by the presidents of North Yemen, the PDRY, and Somalia, which was convened "in order to ensure that the Red Sea remains a lake of peace in the face of big powers [namely, Soviet] involvement."[16]

The efforts to lure South Yemen from the Soviet camp failed (and following the establishment of the Ethiopian-Soviet military alliance, South Yemen became an active supporter of the Derg), and until November 1977, the Somalis were still supplied by the Soviets. But meanwhile, the Riyadh-Cairo-Khartoum axis was cemented, and the Egyptians and the Sudanese coordinated (or at least claimed to coordinate) their military and naval presence in the Red Sea.[17] In April, a representative of the ELF-RC reportedly participated in a joint Egyptian-Sudanese chiefs of staff meeting in Cairo, and the Kuwaitis also declared their full support for the Eritrean struggle.[18]

From the Ethiopian point of view, the emergence of a united Arab Red Sea policy was a nightmare come true. Ethiopian sensitivity to the issue fed on past memories. This semblance of Arab unity in the Red Sea and the bridge it created between the Arabs of the Middle East and the Muslims of the Horn of Africa was unprecedented in modern history. When a similar situation had existed in the early sixteeth century following the establishment of the Otto-man Muslim empire, Ethiopia had been destroyed. At that time under the charismatic leadership of Imam Ahmad ben Ibrahim (nicknamed "Granya"— the "left-handed"), the Somali and Afar Muslims (who were influenced by Muslim holy men from Arabia and were indirectly in touch with Ottoman authorities there) invaded from the Ogaden, conquering and virtually de-stroying the Christian empire (1529–1542). Now as in the past, the Ethiopians were facing a Somali threat, Eritrean victories, and a seemingly united Arab world. To Addis Ababa, "the harsh winds blowing from Syria, Iraq, Kuwait, Saudi Arabia, and Sudan seemed something like a declaration of Jihad."[19] Throughout late 1976 and 1977, the Ethiopian media and official statements portrayed Ethiopia as fighting for survival against Arab reactionaries sup-ported by U.S. imperialism. The Eritreans were, in the words of Mangistu Haila-Mariam, "puppets of imperialists and the reactionary Arab ruling class. Now it is not only their deeds but those of their Arab masters, who testified clearly that their main aim is to hand over Eritrea and the Red Sea to the reactionary Arab governments."[20]

Fortunately for Ethiopia, Mangistu's description of the Eritreans was inaccurate. In 1977, when the Eritreans' old hope of a pro-Eritrean unified Arab policy materialized, the Eritrean nationalist movement was no longer dominated by Arab nationalists. Due to a fundamental transformation in the Eritrean camp (see Chapter Eight), the increasingly Marxist and radically leftist young Eritrean leaders found it unthinkable to identify with Arabism since it was represented by Saudi Arabia, the Sudan, and Egypt. Captives of their newly adopted ideology, the young cadres (especially those of the EPLF) failed to exploit the historic and perhaps unique opportunity of backing their military success with Arab political and financial support. The Red Sea Arabs, led by Saudi Arabia, pinned their hopes on the Pan-Arabist and moderate wing of the Eritrean movement headed by Uthman Salih Sabi. They wanted to see him and others like him lead a unified Eritrean movement, with a concomitant decline in the power of the Marxists and radical leftists. The general trend in the Eritrean movement, however, was moving in exactly the opposite direction—at least as far as the two major organizations were

concerned. Paradoxically, this also prevented internal unity. No less important, it frightened the Red Sea Arabs. In early 1977 the Saudis suspended their
financial support, making renewal conditional on the unification of the two
movements. As it stood, the advocate of unity was Uthman Salih Sabi. The
increasingly leftist EPLF cited Marxist justification for putting revolution
before unity, and its position prevailed.

In early 1977, even as the Eritreans were defeating the Ethiopian army in
the field, they were losing the war. Their old allies and supporters, Libya and
the PDRY (and even the PLO), were now supporting the Derg, and the Soviet
Union and Cuba were about to build a new Ethiopian army. Their potential
new Red Sea allies wished to establish an Arab Eritrea and were reluctant to
support a Marxist revolution. In April, the Saudis made it clear to all Eritrean
organizations that they would not support them until they united.[21] In early
May, the frustrated Uthman Sabi predicted that the Eritreans would be
crushed in three months unless they united and obtained massive Arab
support,[22] but it was a lost cause. By that time, the nonsocialist EDU had
already started to lose ground (it was crushed the following year), and the
Saudis and the Sudanese considered both the EPLF and ELF-RC too radical
to be trusted. By the end of the year, the Sudanese had clearly changed their
minds about an independent Eritrea and started favoring a form of autonomy
under Addis Ababa: "All of us have a vested interest in compromise," a
high-ranking Sudanese official was quoted as saying, "everyone in the region
except the Eritreans."[23]

8.   The Eritrean Movement: "Revolution Before Unity"

Why did the Eritreans miss such a historic opportunity? How could they lose the war while throughout 1975–1977 they had enjoyed military superiority over the Ethiopians and regional circumstances had been so favorable to the establishment of an independent Eritrea?

The reason is to be found primarily in developments within the Eritrean movement. The movement was undergoing profound revolutionary changes, both quantitative and qualitative, yet the old pattern remained unchanged. As in the past, the hard-liners prevailed in the internal struggle for power, leading their organizations in seeming ignorance of the realities of the developing situation. In this they were often encouraged by their young followers. As a result, the movement remained disunited and totally out of step with the intensifying regional and global interference in Horn affairs. Ideological dogmatism grew to dominate policymaking, and the wing calling for "revolution before unity" emerged victorious. The same revolutionary and Marxist commitment also prevented an alliance between the Red Sea Arabs and the Eritrean nationalists. When some former regional allies switched their allegiance in late 1977 to the Ethiopian-Soviet side, the Eritrean movement, though still victorious in the field, remained both disunited and isolated.

An important process in the internal politics of the Eritrean movement during this period was the political decline of the leadership in exile. This stemmed from the quantitative and qualitative growth in the field units of both organizations and the growing political confidence of their commanders. These commanders gained increasing prestige as the result of their military victories, while the exiles in the far-off Arab capitals became increasingly irrelevant. Another major factor in the internal political process was the growing weight of Tigrean Christians, as a new generation of Christian youngsters joined the nationalist forces—primarily the EPLF, but also the ELF-RC. The combined result of these two factors was a rapid erosion of the Arabist component in Eritrean nationalism on the one hand and a growing tendency on the part of the young cadres to adopt leftist radicalism on the other. The exiles, who constituted the bridge to the surrounding Arab world, were thus shunted aside, and the ever-more radical movement became increasingly isolated. The same revolutionary radicalism would also prevent unity—even legitimize disunity—among the leaders in the field. The schisms and rivalries within the Eritrean movement would grow to undermine any military achievement and play further into the hands of the hard-liners on the Ethiopian side.

The first change in the structure of the Eritrean movement since 1972 took place in May 1975 at the Second National Congress of the ELF-RC. This congress, held from 6 May to 27 May in the "liberated areas" between Agordat and Keren, was attended by 949 delegates.

It set up a new 41-member Revolutionary Council and established a 9-member Executive Committee.[1] The old group of exiles led by Idris Adam, Idris Uthman Qladyus, and prominent field commander Heruy Tedla (Tedla Bairu's son), who had dominated the previous council were voted out, for alleged "bourgeois and opportunist" tendencies.[2] The new leadership consisted of those field commanders who had gained prominence at Adobha in 1969, as well as some young members. The 31-year-old Ahmad Nasir, a graduate of the Iraqi military academy and a member of the previous council, was elected the new chairman of both the council and the Executive Committee. Ibrahim Totil, another graduate of the Iraqi military academy and a "pro-Iraqi Ba'thist," was elected vice-chairman of both bodies as well as head of the Political and Organizational Bureau.[3] (A representative of the Iraqi Ba'th Party, a certain Abu Ali, was reportedly an active and influential participant in the congress.[4]) Other prominent members of the new leadership included Az-Zayn Yasin, head of the Foreign Relations Bureau; Abdallah Idris (another pro-Iraqi Ba'thist); Ibrahim Muhammad Ali, head of the Social Affairs Bureau; Abd al-Qadir Ramadan; Muhammad Ibrahim Idris; and young Christians such as Tesfai Walda-Mikael, Malaki Takle (an influential leader in charge of security and a close associate of Ahmad Nasir), and Germai Goshi. (Of the 41 members of the Revolutionary Council, 13 were Christian.[5])

From an ideological point of view, the congress signified a real departure from the First ELF-RC Congress in 1971. The 1975 congress was influenced by younger recruits, many of them Christian Tigrean, who preferred to join the ELF-RC rather than the EPLF as a way to advance the cause of unity between the two organizations.[6] Many of them had defected from the EPLF during the fratricidal 1972–1974 war.[7] It was probably because of the growing weight of this sector that the subject of Eritrean Arabism was virtually ignored, despite the strong Iraqi Ba'thist influence. When it came to the historical interpretation of the Eritrean struggle as "part of the international liberation movement" or to the portrayal of the future revolutionary regime in the independent Eritrea as based on a centralized economy,[8] the resolutions of the congress did not differ much in style and substance from the ideological publications of the rival EPLF. In fact, both organizations were now dominated by people of the same age group who stood for the attainment of the same nationalist and social goals; separating them was a difference of opinion over who would control Eritrea in the future.

However, the operative part of the resolutions dealing with the subject of Eritrean unity signified a major change in concept and tactics. The previous claim that the ELF-RC was the only legitimate representative of the nationalist movement was abandoned. The way to progress as now conceived was no longer by fighting the other organization, but rather by advancing "a democratic dialogue with the [E]PLF, leadership and bases . . . with the objective of realizing the unity of both organizations and establishing one national democratic organization . . . [and] one liberation army."[9] As a result of this congress, the ELF-RC emerged as the wing in the Eritrean movement that emphasized Eritrean unity as a condition for the achievement of military victory and social revolution.

The deposition of his great rival Idris Adam and the ELF-RC's call for Eritrean unity served as a green light for Uthman Salih Sabi, the Beirut-based secretary general of the Foreign Mission of the EPLF. By that time, Uthman was the most vocal representative of Eritrean Arabism in the Arab world. He portrayed himself in the Arab world as the representative of Eritrea, even though he represented only the EPLF. Moreover, his relations with the field commanders, even of his own EPLF, had been tense since late in 1974.[10] The material support he obtained in the Arab world between 1969 and 1974 came mainly from radical, revolutionary Libya, the PDRY, and the PLO. But from 1974 on, Libya and the PDRY started cooperating with the Derg (actively in 1976), while the PLO, decimated in Lebanon, opened an office in Addis Ababa in July 1978.[11] Uthman, however, discerned the emergence of the new Arab Red Sea policy orchestrated by pro-Western Saudi Arabia, Sudan, and Egypt and reoriented his Arab policy. In late 1974 he obtained a promise of support from Saudi Arabia's King Faisal. From that point on, the Red Sea Arabs, considering Uthman as the only leader willing and capable of leading an Arab Eritrea, channeled most of their support through him. Carrying this precious dowry of arms and money, Uthman attempted to unify the Eritrean movement under his non-Marxist and Arab-oriented leadership.[12]

In June 1975, Uthman started negotiating with the new leaders of the ELF-RC, especially Az-Zayn Yasin and Abdallah Idris. In July, when the Sudanese stopped their aid to the ELF-RC, Ahmad Nasir, desperate for a new source of supplies, also joined the process.[13] Negotiations were conducted throughout July and August in Baghdad and Beirut, culminating in a week-long meeting in Khartoum (2–8 September 1975). There, under the auspices of Iraqi mediators, the EPLF Foreign Mission was represented by all its prominent members: head of the mission Walda-Ab Walda-Mariam, Muhammad Said Nawud, Taha Muhammad Nur, and Secretary General Uthman Sabi.[14] According to an ELF-RC publication, Uthman and his friends claimed to represent the whole of the EPLF and even presented a document authorizing them to do so.[15]

The meeting ended with a resolution that seemingly promised nationalist unity within a short period. It was decided that a 24-member committee would start preparations in two months for a unification conference to be held during 1976. Meanwhile, joint coordinating committees were to be established to deal with foreign affairs, military operations, and political and social affairs. A separate 12-man central coordinating committee would oversee their work. It was also decided that all foreign military, financial, and other assistance to the movement would be divided equally between the organizations. Indeed, in October 1975, for the first time in the history of the Eritrean struggle, a unified delegation, led by Ahmad Nasir and Uthman Salih Sabi, toured Arab capitals.[16] An organ of the ELF-RC described the resolutions as "positive and major steps in the direction . . . of establishing complete unity, based on the objectives and principles of the revolution, between the two liberation movements."[17] In practice, however, they turned out to be only the beginning of a long and complex political process marred by growing antagonisms and internal conflicts.

By mid-1975, relations between Uthman Sabi and the military command of the EPLF (the Administrative Committee) had broken down; in fact, there had been little contact between EPLF fighters and the Foreign Mission since late 1974. The split between the two wings of the organization was not over questions of leadership since from the start a clear functional division of power and tasks had been created: Uthman was to collect funds abroad, while Isayas and his associates were to lead the fighters in the field. There was a major argument over the question of distributing the movement's funds,[18] but it arose only as a result of a fundamental split, apparently over ideology and regional orientation. While Marxism continued to prevail in the field, due to the influence of Eritrean students' organizations affiliated with the EPLF both in the United States and in Western Europe, Uthman was portrayed as a petit bourgeois, a servant of the Saudis, and eventually as an agent of imperialism and Zionism.[19] His signing of a unity agreement with the ELF-RC in the name of the EPLF created an open split in the organization. When the military commanders of the EPLF received a letter sent by the ELF-RC about the September 1975 Khartoum agreement, they responded that "they knew nothing of any agreement between the ELF and official representatives of the [E]PLF."[20] A delegation sent by the Foreign Mission to discuss the matter with the EPLF cadres in the field returned empty-handed. On 2 November 1975, an EPLF group representing the "northern coast" published its rejection of the Khartoum agreement. Uthman's efforts to re-establish contact with the EPLF Administrative Committee proved fruitless. It was only in March 1976 that the leaders of the two wings of the EPLF met in Khartoum. Discussions were held in a cold atmosphere (18–23 March). Of the fighters in the field only Muhammad Umar Abdallah, the commander of the Massawiyun, was ready to accept the unity agreement with the ELF-RC. The rest refused even to discuss the matter. Following the collapse of the negotiations, both sides announced officially that relations had been cut. Two days later the Foreign Mission published the long "Important Message to the Eritrean People" (signed by Uthman, Idris Adam, Muhammad Said Nawud, Muhammad al-Burj, and Taha Nur) analyzing the situation in the Eritrean movement and blaming the EPLF Administrative Committee for recklessly blowing a historic opportunity to unite the Eritrean nation. On 28 March Isayas Afawarq, in the name of "the leadership of the EPLF," published a leaflet strongly denouncing the Foreign Mission as "imposing a kind of a unity that would serve first of all the interest of the Foreign Mission and enable it to continue the imposition of an absolute guardianship on the Eritrean Revolution." He announced that "the former Foreign Mission no longer represents the [E]PLF as of 23 March, 1976 . . . It no longer has the right to speak in the name of the [E]PLF. We call on all friends to stop dealing with what used to be called the Foreign Mission and to support the interests of the Eritrean masses represented by the [E]PLF."[21]

From that point, Uthman became the hated enemy of the EPLF and was regarded as a traitor. It became unthinkable for the EPLF to contemplate any form of unity including Uthman. Furthermore, while Uthman and the ELF-RC called for unity as a precondition to a nationalist victory, the EPLF rejected such a "reactionary line of immediate merger." Leaders of the ELF-RC and Uthman were dismissed as "feudalist compradors and bureaucratic capitalists," who rather than being counted partners to national unity had to be destroyed by forces of the revolution. "At no time," an EPLF publication asserted, "has the EPLF called for the merger of the two fronts . . . it has consistently and vehemently opposed this reactionary line which is peddled by the ELF leadership. Time and again the EPLF has pointed out that those who advance this reactionary line and those who advise the Eritrean people to follow this erroneous road to the unity are either . . . antipeople forces . . . or are forces who fail to realize that such artificial unity would only serve the purpose of our primary enemy."[22]

Indeed, the EPLF, standing for "revolution as a precondition to unity," seemed to have good practical reasons to delay unity and condition it on the ill-defined (at least, temporarily ill-defined) concept of revolution. During the battles against the Ethiopians, it became apparent that the EPLF units were far better trained and better motivated than those of the ELF-RC. They were made up of better-educated, Christian town dwellers and had also accumulated more combat experience (after the Ethiopian army evacuated most of the ELF-RC area in western Eritrea, the EPLF bore the brunt of the fighting). Confident that the EPLF would govern in an independent Eritrea, the group adopted the Maoist approach of "people's war, that is to say: liberate the land piece by piece [and then] establish and consolidate people's authority step by step, for in the final analysis, the national struggle is a class struggle."[23]

In governing and organizing the population in the territories it occupied, the EPLF was impressively successful. During 1975 and 1976 it gained control over rural areas east of Keren (with the exception of some ELF-RC enclaves in Afar country and south of Asmara) and in 1977 captured several towns, including Karora, Naqfa, and Decamere. The EPLF proceeded to carry out revolutionary changes in these "liberated areas," including the introduction of local land reforms; the establishment of schools, hospitals, and local factories; the construction of roads; the establishment of locally managed transport companies; the publication of newspapers and other means of ideological indoctrination; and intensive military training and indoctrination of teenagers.[24]

Successful and efficient, EPLF leaders seemed to be marching confidently toward implementing a social revolution leading, as they conceived it, toward nationalist liberation, while at the same time securing for themselves the government of the future state. Unity with the ELF-RC and the Foreign Mission before achieving this final victory was conceived as compromising on both ideology and power. It was for these reasons that young EPLF cadres rejected Uthman Sabi and his "reactionary Saudi money."[25] It was also for these reasons that political unity with the ELF-RC was not achieved during this period.

With the EPLF rejection of Uthman Sabi and the Foreign Mission, the Khartoum agreement of September 1975 was rendered meaningless. The leaders of the ELF-RC had only very sketchy information about political developments in the EPLF.[26] They did, however, persistently call for "unity before independence." The natural step would have been to accept all prominent Eritrean leaders as partners in the future united leadership. "We do not share the EPLF objection to Uthman Sabi's inclusion in the Front," Ahmad Nasir said. "He might be a conservative, but he certainly is not the traitor the

EPLF leaders call him."[27] In July 1976, the ELF-RC recognized the Foreign Mission as a third organization in the Eritrean movement.[28] The following month, the ELF-RC again stressed the importance of unity among the three organizations and proclaimed the formation of a new committee to establish contact with the EPLF with the aim of organizing a joint congress.[29]

Although some military cooperation between the combat units of the EPLF and ELF-RC was reluctantly maintained throughout 1976, the EPLF remained clearly evasive about eventual political unity. The increasingly confident leaders bided their time. In June 1976 they started preparing for the long-awaited First Organizational Congress of the EPLF, an event that took place some seven months later, between 23 and 31 January 1977.

The EPLF congress, held in the "liberated areas," was attended by hundreds of delegates from combat units and other branches of the organization, as well as from foreign countries. It resulted in the adoption of an eleven-point program on the nature of the regime in the future Eritrean state, which was to be directed by a revolutionary socialist regime. The innovation in ideology, however, was the clear departure from Arabism and the emphasis on the pluralist nature of Eritrean society. Thus, a new insignia was adopted by the organization: nine bullets, symbolizing the nine languages spoken in the country.[30]

From an organizational point of view, a new structure was proposed. The EPLF would be headed by a Central Committee of 43 members elected for two years. The executive body would be a Political Bureau, made up of the top 13 members of the Central Committee.[31] Ramadan Muhammad Nur was re-elected secretary general of the organization, with Isayas Afawarq as his deputy. As would later become clear, these two were not in full harmony on the question of unity with the ELF-RC.

Two other resolutions regarding unity were of great significance. The first resolution was to rename the organization the Eritrean People's Liberation Front. The change from *forces* to *front* was probably a strong indication that the EPLF saw itself as being the true, possibly the only, representative of the Eritreans (a concept previously adopted but later abandoned by the rival ELF). The second relevant resolution dealt with policy toward other organizations. Essentially the resolution legitimized the existing line—the Foreign Mission was totally rejected as a nationalist organization. As for unity with the ELF-RC, it was resolved that it had to be "handled gradually" and had to pass through a "united front" stage—that is, a "united front" would be a framework to advance "coordination of field operations and information" while each group maintained "its identity." Such a stage was "a prerequisite to lasting unity."[32]

The Central Committee met immediately after the congress (and again on 7 May 1977) to draft a detailed program along the line of the resolutions. The program gave absolute priority (over the matter of unity) to the issues of military liberation and of social revolution in the "liberated areas."[33]

In the meantime, Uthman Sabi did not sit passively. With almost unlimited financial resources by Eritrean standards, he started recruiting fighters from the two other organizations and from among Eritrean refugees in the Sudan. By early 1977, he had already mobilized some two thousand men, who based themselves in the northwestern regions of Eritrea. When the battles started in the Eritrean towns, Uthman again called for unity, promising that the much-needed heavy weaponry would be supplied by his Arab friends.[34]

Uthman, his money, and his arms were nevertheless strongly rejected by the EPLF, which, quoting extensively from Chairman Mao, announced: "We will not barter our principles for a mess of potage. Self-reliance in all fields of revolutionary activity is the underlying basis for the proper execution of our political line."[35] At the same time, although Uthman was recognized by the official leadership of the ELF-RC, other, strongly Marxist-oriented, mostly Christian factions within this organization violently opposed any cooperation with the "reactionary" Uthman. Thus, the relentless veteran had to establish a new organization, made up of his forces in the field and the Foreign Mission, which he named the Eritrean Liberation Front–Popular Liberation Forces (ELF-PLF), apparently to symbolize his firm position on unity. In April 1977, Uthman chaired the First Organizational Congress of his ELF-PLF "in the liberated areas" near Agordat.[36] It resolved to form a united nationalist movement based on mutual recognition of the three existing organizations, with this fact suitably reflected in the leadership. It also sharpened the ideological differences, particularly with the EPLF, by calling for relations with the neighboring Arabs to be strengthened and the establishment of a "free, secular and democratic state, based on Eritrean needs and situations, and not on slogans quoted from books."[37]

The establishment of the ELF-PLF during a period marked by unprecedented military victories by the Eritreans only emphasized the harmful internal disunity in the movement. "The nearer we get to independence," said a frustrated member of the Revolutionary Council, "the less chance there is for unity."[38] Eritrean leaders seemed to take victory for granted and focused their attention on their own internal struggle for power. A Western journalist who spent weeks interviewing Eritreans in the field produced a gloomy picture of splits and intrigues; he concluded that the basic differences were less a matter of ideology than of personal rivalries cloaked in ideological phraseology.[39]

Both the Saudis and the Iraqis started pressuring the Eritreans to unite. The Saudis clearly conditioned renewal of support on unity,[40] and the Iraqis' expression of support for Uthman Sabi was an apparent attempt to encourage their associates in the ELF-RC to work harder for this aim. Uthman himself spared no effort to emphasize, time and again, that a military victory prior to unification of the movement would be disastrous: "The splits will bring about [following the victory] an Eritrean civil war, which will, as was the case in Angola, enable foreigners from the West or from the East, even the Israelis, to intervene."[41]

During June and July 1977, when Eritrean victories in the field culminated in the capture of Keren and Decamere, it seemed as if foreign pressure on the Eritreans to unite might prove fruitful. By that time, Ethiopia was making new and intensive efforts to rebuild its army. In late May 1977, a dialogue had started between the EPLF and ELF-RC, which led to an agreement in Khartoum on 5 June 1977 to work toward establishing a National Democratic Front, conceived, as stipulated by the EPLF congress of January, as "a prerequisite to a lasting unity." Paradoxically the front was to include— or at least, this was the EPLF's position—two non-Eritrean organizations, the TPLF and the EPRP.[42] At the same time, on the EPLF's insistence, the ELF-PLF was excluded. The ELF-RC, however, made it clear that its dialogue with the ELF-PLF would continue.

Between 24 and 27 July, negotiations were held in Eritrea between an ELF-RC delegation headed by Ibrahim Totil and an ELF-PLF delegation headed by Muhammad Said Nawud. The two sides reached an agreement that stipulated that the ELF-PLF was to join the National Democratic Front. This significant step toward unity between the ELF-RC and the ELF-PLF also meant the unification of their fighting units in the field. Both organizations now declared that they were ready for talks with the EPLF on "comprehensive national unity." "We have been here for more than three weeks," Uthman Sabi announced from the site of the talks, "waiting for the EPLF leader Isayas Afawarq [to come and sign] in order that we [can] unite the fighting units and liberate the ports of Assab and Massawa."[43]

These developments only served to make the disunity more visible. An important factor in this was the growing political power of the young cadres in both the ELF-RC and the EPLF at the expense of the authority of the recognized leaders. In early 1975, the rank and file had managed to impose a sort of unity. Now their activity helped to create confusion and splits. This was particularly the case in the ELF-RC. Since September 1975, leftist groups in this organization, consisting mainly of Christian highlanders, had violently opposed their leaders' cooperation with Uthman Sabi. Some even revolted openly and established contact with EPLF units.[44] By July 1977, the ELF-RC was internally torn over the question of national unity. Clashes between rival factions even claimed the life of prominent ELF-RC member Abd al-Qadir Ramadan, who had been in charge of information. Some of the action was attributed to subversive efforts by the EPLF.

During July some two hundred members of the ELF-RC were killed. A further twelve hundred left the organization, mostly after the agreement with

Uthman's ELF-PLF. They renamed themselves the ELF–Democratic Forces; the ELF-RC called them *fallul* (roughly equivalent to "anarchist"). Another fifteen hundred members defected to the EPLF during the subsequent two or three months. Still others, especially ELF-RC members from the coastal areas of Afar, established a group called Majmu' al-Tashih and called for a full merger with the ELF-PLF even at the expense of future compromise with the EPLF. In June, Heruy Tedla-Bairu, who in May 1975 had been removed from power for being a "reactionary," established "a Marxist organization" in opposition to the ELF-RC. Against this background, there were speculations that relations between Ahmad Nasir and his two closest associates, Ibrahim Totil and Abdallah Idris, were affected by these problems within the organization.[45]

The EPLF was experiencing similar problems. It was reported, for instance, that the organization had arrested some seven hundred of its members in July for resisting the official line on national unity (and also because of other internal problems, such as relations between various regional and ethnic groups).[46] More important, mutual suspicion and distrust between the ELF-RC and the EPLF grew with their military victories over the Ethiopian army. The June 1977 agreement on the National Democratic Front also stipulated equal distribution of weapons captured from the Ethiopians. When Keren fell to the EPLF the following month, the ELF-RC (particularly annoyed since this important town had previously been considered within its sphere of influence) demanded its share, but this was apparently denied them. The ELF-RC's reaction was to accuse the EPLF of plotting with the Derg and the Soviets against Eritrean nationalism. The logic of such cooperation, they alleged, was that both the Derg and the EPLF adopted a Marxist approach, advocating a federal solution to Horn affairs. The proof of their suspicions, they said, was the inexplicable ease with which the EPLF had captured Keren. It was a simple deal, alleged the ELF-RC. The Ethiopians gave Keren to the EPLF, and the EPLF avoided uniting with the ELF-RC to capture the ports of Massawa and Assab. As a result of these accusations, military cooperation between the ELF-RC and the EPLF came to an end.[47]

Thus, while the Somalis were invading the Ogaden, theoretically enabling the Eritreans to fortify their positions, the Eritrean organizations were disunited and mutually hostile. The ELF-RC and the ELF-PLF finally made a token effort at cooperation, and in the middle of September 1977 they claimed to have captured the town of Agordat together.[48] This was, however, quite insignificant since in terms of fighting ability the practical power of the ELF-PLF was meaningless. Uthman Sabi, though, was confident of his diplomatic position in the region as a whole: "If we proclaim the establishment of an independent state, we would, beyond any doubt, win the respect and the active support . . . of the Arab states."[49] But this could not be achieved without the EPLF.

In August 1977, after concluding the agreement with the ELF-PLF, Ahmad Nasir, the leader of the ELF-RC, left for Damascus to conduct negotiations with EPLF Secretary General Ramadan Nur. By that time, the EPLF had started feeling the pressure of regional isolation, and even the prominent hard-liner Isayas Afawarq left to tour such "reactionary countries" as Saudi Arabia, the Sudan, Abu Dhabi, and Kuwait.[50] In Damascus, under the auspices of their Ba'thist hosts, Ramadan and Ahmad Nasir reportedly reached an agreement, but EPLF cadres in the field were to reverse Ramadan's decisions.[51] The negotiations were resumed, this time with Isayas representing the EPLF. On 20 October 1977, Isayas signed an agreement with Ahmad Nasir in Khartoum revitalizing the idea of a national democratic front. The two parties decided to form a joint political leadership and joint committees on military, information, economic, social, and foreign affairs, "while retaining their political and organizational independence." They also agreed to start preparing for a unity congress. This time, however, Uthman Sabi's ELF-PLF was to be sacrificed. Under pressure from Isayas, Nasir agreed to revoke the ELF-RC's recognition of the ELF-PLF as an official Eritrean organization.[52]

This proved to be just another futile exercise. Throughout November, EPLF and ELF-RC units clashed around Elaberet. In the third week of November 1977, when the 43-member Central Committee of the EPLF met to discuss the agreement, it was apparently strongly criticized by representatives of the rank and file. The Central Committee decided that further negotiation with the ELF-RC should aim only "to bring about a unity that satisfies the interests and aspirations of the masses." When the leaders of both organizations reconvened (27–30 November 1977), the EPLF forced a decision to establish merely "a united front with separate leaderships and organizations."[53]

This was, in fact, the end of the process. The EPLF boycotted the next meeting, scheduled for mid-December, and the leaders of the two organizations did not meet again before March 1978. Instead, they launched a campaign of mutual accusations. On 27 December, the ELF-RC spokesman in Rome admitted that the agreement was void.[54]

On the threshold of victory, after occupying most of Eritrea, the young leaders had lost their chance to implement their goals. They had pushed aside the experienced older leaders in exile, but their radicalism prevented them from benefiting from what was fundamentally a pro-Eritrean process in the region. Libya and the PDRY now supported the Soviet-oriented Derg, while the contribution of the PLO steadily diminished. The neighboring Red Sea Arab states conceived an independent, radical Eritrea as a great threat to their interests. Thus, the stronger the EPLF became, the more isolated it became. It lost almost all its foreign aid following the split with the Foreign Mission in early 1976. The ELF-RC, on the other hand, continued to enjoy the verbal (though in practice insignificant) support of far-off Ba'thist Iraq. The ELF-PLF, despite Arab financial support, was virtually meaningless in terms of fighting ability in the field. Captives of their own rivalries and dependent on the cadres they had raised, the young leaders of the Eritrean organizations were unable to unite. Toward the end of 1977, the growing fear of a renewal of the 1971–1974 fratricidal war was the main factor behind the Eritrean hesitation to try to capture Asmara.[55] The leaders of the two main organizations had good reason to foresee an Angola-like battle between them once full liberation was achieved. And so, while the Ethiopian army was occupied in the Ogaden, the Eritreans did little to exploit their unique opportunity.

In 1978 the Eritreans resumed their efforts at unification. In early March some fruitless talks were held in Khartoum;[56] then, between 22 and 24 April 1978, the joint political leadership and the five joint committees of the National Democratic Front, whose establishment had been agreed in October 1977, finally convened at Keren. It was decided to resume military cooperation between the EPLF and the ELF-RC and to form a committee to start preparing for a national congress. The committee was to report on its work after six months. The ELF-PLF was again denied recognition, and its members were presented with an ultimatum to join one of the organizations or face destruction.[57] Uthman Sabi categorically rejected the ultimatum and continued to call for unity on the basis of equality among the three organizations.[58] In the field, military cooperation continued to be problematic and plagued by mutual suspicions.[59]

By the second part of 1978 the Eritreans had lost their opportunity to unite as victors. In the moment of truth, the Eritreans failed to pull together in the name of Eritreanism. The reality of ethnic, religious, regional, social, and personal rivalries couched in revolutionary phraseology legitimizing disunity proved stronger that the relatively young sentiment of Eritrean nationalism. Meanwhile, in Ethiopia—in contrast—hierarchical centralism was to prevail over centrifugal tendencies; since April 1977, Ethiopia had been undergoing an intensive process of mobilization, and its state machinery and armed forces were being rebuilt. In early 1978, only one issue remained to be settled: Could the Eritreans, after failing to unite in the face of success, unite in the face of defeat?

9. The Ethiopian Revolution: "Unity or Death"

The configuration in the region following the 1974 revolution in Ethiopia tended to favor the Eritrean separatists. The Ethiopian state machinery had crumbled. The increasingly strong Red Sea Arabs had become interested in an Arab Eritrea. In the province itself nationalist sentiments had increased, and the military ability of the Eritrean organizations now far exceeded that of the Ethiopian units they were facing. Yet the Eritreans failed to exploit the opportunity, primarily because of the ascendancy of the wing that called for "revolution before unity." In Addis Ababa, in contrast, a bitter, often brutal, intensive internal struggle led to the supremacy of the "unity or death" faction. "Unity" in this case referred to the territorial integrity of Mother Ethiopia; the victorious side was prepared to sacrifice everything to achieve it. This willingness to sacrifice all was perhaps why so little was done to solve the problem politically. Yet this was also why Ethiopia emerged strong enough in early 1978 to recapture Eritrean towns and to frustrate the Eritreans' aspirations to fulfill their nationalism at the expense of Ethiopia's integrity.

Three years earlier, in late 1974, such developments had seemed unthinkable. The Ethiopia that emerged in 1974 lacked functional leadership; the soldiers and officers in the Derg could hardly maintain control over the capital, let alone run a state. They had difficulty coming to decisions on any matter of importance. Because of the collegial structure of the Derg (which resulted from the events of 1974 rather than from a calculated plan), every discussion became a struggle for power and influence. From the start, the Eritrean question was a major issue in this struggle—perhaps the most crucial one. The political competition in the Derg was such that losers often paid with their lives, and the struggle over Eritrea was a major factor in the process of elimination from which Mangistu Haila-Mariam emerged as the ruler of the Derg.

There was no ideological dispute in the Derg over the matter of Eritrean nationalism; it was totally denied. The slogan of "Ethiopia First" with its territorial interpretation reflected a consensus that recognition of any separatism would lead to total dismemberment. Following the events of 1974, it became increasingly difficult to defeat Eritrean separatism, but it became ever more vital to do so. Ignoring the subject would no longer do. This required the adoption of a consistent policy, and it was this that led to three years of wrangling in the Derg.

From a practical point of view, the developments in Ethiopia in 1974 meant primarily the destruction of the state machinery built by Haile Selassie. The NCOs and low-ranking officers who were the country's new rulers deposed the politicians, generals, and administrators of the old political establishment but were unable to offer an adequate system in its place. As a result, the civil administration stopped functioning, while the army, deprived of its higher commanders, underwent a process of politicization, which weakened it still further militarily. Administrative control over the various provinces ceased in all but name, and local revolts in virtually all of them compounded the problem. The regime tried to reassert central control and to rebuild the administration through the implementation of a land-reform program and the formation of tens of thousands of peasants' associations. However, this attempt did not include Eritrea, and official publications dealing with such subjects did not mention the name of the troubled province.[1] The Eritrean-based 2d Division was politicized even more than other army units; while the Derg was able to break up committees in battalions based near the center, the soldiers in distant, war-stricken Eritrea maintained their committees throughout.[2] Bearing the brunt of what became a defensive war, the committees of the 2d Division now pressed for a political solution, in contrast to the tough stance the 2d Division took in Ethiopia before the revolution. (Reinforcement from the 1st Division and other forces made only a small difference in this respect.)

In the Derg itself, the arguments over Eritrea—as always, an integral part of what was essentially a struggle for power (and physical survival)—focused on tactics to be used against the separatists. As in the past, the division was between those who sought a political solution and those who supported a military one.

From the outset, Maj. Mangistu Haila-Mariam was the most vocal supporter of the military option. Mangistu had brought about the fall of Aman Andom and the appointment of the hard-liner Tafari Banti as chairman of the PMAC, and his power in the Derg rested on a small group of supporting officers (such as Berhanu Bayeh, Endale Tesamma, Getachaw Shibeshi, Demisse Darassa, and Nadaw Zakariyas) and on the support of the majority of the NCOs. The majority of his supporters—NCOs as well as officers—were said to be from the southern provinces. They were either of Oromo origin or descendants of the old *naftanya* families—soldier-settlers who came from the north during the late nineteenth century conquest of southern Ethiopia and integrated with local society. Mangistu himself was of mixed origin and was widely considered to be a sworn enemy of the old Amhara ruling class. It was for this reason that some speculated, though never convincingly, that Derg members from the north inclined toward a political solution in the northern province, while the Oromos and other southerners tended to be less patient with the Eritreans and favored the military option. (Some hard-liners in the Derg reportedly advocated not only an all-out war against the Eritrean organizations, but also the mass transfer of Eritreans to Ethiopia and the settlement of southerners in the northern province.) What was, however, clear from the start was that Major (from November 1976, Lieutenant Colonel) Mangistu supported a very hard line against those undermining Ethiopia's integrity. It was in a speech against Aman in November 1974 that he first declared his slogan "Unity or Death," and it was by eliminating his opponents in an effort to achieve unity that he emerged after three years of struggle as the ruler of the Derg.

But in 1975 and 1976, Mangistu was far from being all-powerful in this collegial council. In the struggle for power and influence, Mangistu's leftist rivals—notably, Captains Sisai Habte, Alamayhu Haile, and Mogus Walda-Mikael—adopted a different policy. They attributed greater importance to revolution than to unity, seeing the latter as an ultimate outcome of the former. They therefore emphasized the social aspects of the revolution, on sharing power with leftist civilians and seeking a political solution in Eritrea. It was due to their influence that on 16 May 1976 the Derg published its Nine-Point Plan for achieving such a solution in Eritrea.

The Nine-Point Plan stemmed from a more general program to rebuild the regime in Ethiopia along the lines of "scientific socialism." The general approach, which dated back to early 1975, was supplemented by a detailed program entitled the National Democratic Revolution adopted by the Derg on 20 April 1976.[3] In essence it stipulated the establishment of a politically centralized one-party people's republic made up of various ethnic, linguistic, and other groups that would enjoy self-administration in many regions. "The People's Democratic Republic of Ethiopia," according to this program, "would be established under the leadership of the proletariat . . . to guarantee to the Ethiopian people their right to freedom, equality, unity, peace, and prosperity, as well as *self-administration at various levels* and unrestricted human and democratic rights [italics added]."

As for the nature of the proposed self-administration, the program asserted: "Under the prevailing conditions in Ethiopia the problem of nationalities can only be solved when the nationalities are guaranteed regional autonomy. Accordingly, each nationality will have the right to decide on matters prevailing within its environs, be they administrative, political, economic, social or language, as well as elect its own leaders and administrators."

The implications of the program for the Eritrean problem were clear. On the one hand, Eritrea, like the other provinces, would for all practical purposes cease to exist. (Earlier in 1975, "administrative region" [*kifle hagar*] had replaced "province" [*taklay gezat*].) On the other hand, districts in Eritrea were to enjoy self-administration—although in accordance with the concept of nationality, some of them were probably to be merged with districts in neighboring Tigre, Wallo, or Bagemdir provinces. According to the *Ethiopian Herald* of 7 May 1976, the population of Eritrea was to be divided among seven such national districts. Implementation, however, was postponed to the remote future. The immediate policy, presented in the Nine-Point Plan, based on decisions taken by the Derg with regard to Eritrea and "in accordance with the Ethiopian National Democratic Revolution Program," may be summarized as follows:

1. Full participation by the people of the Eritrean administrative region in the country's political, economic, and social movements, with the rest of the Ethiopian people, by abolishing the previous inefficient and inequitable situation. In particular, the people of Eritrea would share fully and participate in the struggle to form the people's democratic republic.

2. Regional autonomy would be granted all nationalities in Ethiopia. In order to implement their right of self-determination, the government would submit the findings of a study of the geography, administration, and development of the regions. The self-determination decision would be taken by all the Ethiopian people.

3. The PMAC would give immediate autonomy to the people of the Eritrean administrative region in collaboration with progressive forces and was ready to discuss the immediate implementation of this with the progressive forces, in order to solve the Eritrean problem peacefully.

4. The government would give full support to progressive forces in Eritrea in their struggle to crush the three enemies of the Ethiopian people—namely, feudalism, bureaucratic-capitalism, and imperialism—in collaboration with the progressive forces of the rest of the Ethiopian people.

5. The government would immediately begin to give any necessary assistance for the return of all Ethiopians who had fled to other countries because of the Eritrean problems.

6. The government would make special efforts to rehabilitate those who had lost property. In addition, efforts would be made to find jobs or schools for those, in any region of the country, who had lost their jobs or discontinued their studies.

7. Political prisoners would be released. However, those sentenced to life imprisonment or death would either be released or have their sentences reduced as soon as peace prevailed, according to the gravity of their crime.

8. The state of emergency in Eritrea would be lifted when peace prevailed there and when the major points mentioned above were in the process of implementation.

9. A special commission for the Eritrean administrative region would be established by decree[4] and would work on the implementation of points five to seven.[5]

The adoption and publication of the plan reflected the strength of the Marxist-oriented wing in the Derg and of others who favored a political solution in Eritrea. Their hope was that the EPLF (undoubtedly the "progressive forces of Eritrea" referred to in the program) would go along with the plan. Indeed, at its January 1977 congress, the EPLF adopted the idea of self-administration for what it defined as the "nine nationalities of Eritrea." (The subsequent EPLF statement was the first recognition by Eritrean nationalists that there was a nationality issue in Eritrea.[6]) The difference, of course, was that the EPLF wanted self-administration within an Eritrean *state*, while the Derg program implied the abolition of Eritrea even as an administrative entity.

For this reason the publication of the plan was nothing more than an academic exercise and, as such, not necessarily a defeat for the hard-liners headed by Mangistu and the second vice-chairman of the Derg, Lt. Col. Atnafu Abate. Mangistu had learned to exploit Marxist concepts to make tactical power gains. For him the program was a good cover, giving a facade of high political purpose to the military plans he had for Eritrea. The plan, which was warmly accepted by many African states and communist countries, was promptly and flatly rejected by the Eritrean organizations.

While the Derg was waving this olive branch with one hand, its other hand, the wing headed by Mangistu and Atnafu, was preparing the Peasants March—the military option. The person in charge of its organization was Lt. Col. Atnafu Abate. Since 1974, when Atnafu had helped establish the Derg, he had been a prominent contender for its leadership. He derived his influence both from his position as a leader in the capital-based 4th Division and from his role as organizer of militia forces in the various provinces, a process that started in 1975. These militia forces were to serve as auxiliary units in case of external war, quell local revolts, help restore authority, and rebuild the state machinery throughout the country. The peasant army organized by Atnafu against Eritrea in March 1976 was a combined force drawn from the militias of Tigre, Bagemdir, and Wallo. The failure of this march heavily damaged Atnafu's position and, to a lesser extent, Mangistu's prestige.

Yet, in retrospect, this was an important episode in the history of the entire region. First, the Derg learned a lesson: provincial militia forces lacking training, adequate arms, and motivation born of indoctrination were not enough. The old army was worn out and too small to cope with the growing challenges confronting Ethiopia. Recruiting students and young members of urban communities could further politicize the armed forces. The leftist and Marxist wing in the Derg, many of whose members served in the more technologically sophisticated units, favored this option. Paradoxically, this implied strengthening relations with the United States, the army's major supplier. The wing led by Mangistu and Atnafu, in contrast, preferred another option—one that would be realized within a year and a half and revolutionize the whole situation in the Horn—the massive recruitment of hundreds of thousands of peasants, mainly from the southern areas (where the revolution was more widely accepted), into a national militia. This new army would later not only provide an adequate response to the external challenges, but also serve as the foundation for a new state machinery loyal to its builders. However, the training of these new forces did not begin until April 1977.

Second, it was apparently following the failure of the Peasants March (though not immediately) that Mangistu oriented his policy toward the Soviet Union. Even before the peasants set foot on Eritrean soil, Washington had applied heavy pressure on the Derg to call off the campaign. By that time it had become apparent that the United States would not agree to massively rearm Ethiopia—especially when the army in question was to be a huge Maoist-type peasant army such as Mangistu and his associates had long envisioned. It may even be assumed that Mangistu had wanted the Soviets from the start. Under the circumstances, although still the main supplier of the Ethiopian professional army, the United States became a reluctant and increasingly reserved supporter. Despite a U.S. commitment to sell arms to Ethiopia until 1978, the Pentagon's regard for Ethiopia's strategic importance had declined. Following the closure of the Suez Canal, Kaganew—the U.S. communication and intelligence-gathering base at Asmara—seemed to lose importance: the number of Americans at the base declined from some three thousand in the 1960s to no more than several hundred in 1974. Too much risk was involved in maintaining a base in the heart of war-troubled Eritrea, and in any case in 1974 a more sophisticated base was built on the Indian Ocean island of Diego Garcia. In 1978 Kaganew was shut down.

After the revolution, relations between Addis Ababa and Washington changed course. When all important members of the previous establishment were executed without trial on 23 November 1974, Washington reacted by announcing that it was suspending all military and economic assistance to Ethiopia. In early 1975, when open war broke out in Eritrea, the Derg requested prompt delivery of $25–27 million worth of ammunition, but Washington was reluctant. Both states were mutually suspicious.[7] Although the United States resumed the supply of arms and continued delivering substantial quantities until late in the summer of 1976,[8] it viewed the growing radicalism and increasing brutality in Addis Ababa with concern. The Derg's young officers, for their part, identified the United States with the corruption of the previous regime on the one hand and with the rising cause of Arabism in the Red Sea on the other. Moreover, it was rumored that Mangistu himself harbored bitterness toward the United States because of a racist insult he had experienced during a short stay in a U.S. military academy. Washington's rejection of the Peasants March on the grounds of its barbarism[9] was apparently the ultimate proof for Mangistu (if indeed he needed one) that he must reorient his policy. The United States would never help him arm a popular army of hundreds of thousands of indoctrinated peasants. At best it might continue to aid the professional army, thus playing into the hands of his rivals. He arrived at a paradoxical solution: he would use the Soviet Union to defeat his leftist, Marxist opponents.

But until early 1977, Mangistu was not in a position to force implementation of his line. In fact, after the fiasco of the Peasants March, his position, and that of Atnafu, was weakened. Their rivals were strong enough to try to advance their casue.

Ranked number three in the Derg was Capt. Sisai Habte, the chairman of the Derg's Political and Foreign Affairs Committee. He was a university-educated air force officer of Gurage origin. During the 1974 developments, he headed a revolutionary committee at the Dabra-Zait air base and as such played a prominent role in the establishment of the Derg and the creation of the revolution. Sisai was said to be a Marxist by ideology but a pragmatist by policy. His interests in the internal struggle lay in strengthening the standing army, the air force, and other professional units, and thus he became the architect of resuming relations with Western states. Since relations with the United States remained guarded, the only real option was Israel.

In early 1975, when the Eritrean separatists, aided by the Arabs, turned the conflict into an open war, the Derg turned to Israel and expressed regrets for Haile Selassie's cutting of relations.[10] According to a report included in a publication issued by Uthman Salih Sabi, it was Captain Sisai who then left for Israel to negotiate the resumption of Israeli aid.[11] Although there was no resumption of diplomatic relations, the renewed practical relations were no less significant than those of the late 1960s. By 1975, Israel had responded to the Arab challenge in the Red Sea by developing a small fleet of highly sophisticated missile boats. According to the Eritrean separatists and the Arab press, these boats were allowed to refuel at the Ethiopian Red Sea islands of Halib and Fatima as well as at the port of Assab and the islands of Dahlak, Zukar, and Hanish.[12] In return for this service, indeed out of a common interest of preventing the establishment of an Arab Eritrea, Israel supplied desperately needed ammunition and spare parts for the Ethiopian army's U.S. equipment. At the same time, the Israelis helped the Ethiopians build new units for the regular army. According to Eritrean sources, a group of some ten Israeli officers began training the new 5th Division, the Flame Division (*Nebalbal*), in 1975.[13] Brigades from this division participated in battles in Eritrea from mid-1976 on. Relations between Israel and Ethiopia survived until early 1978 despite Soviet pressure on the Derg throughout 1977 to terminate them; it was only the accidental public exposure of the existence of such relations in February 1978 by Israeli Foreign Minister Moshe Dayan that led the Derg to cut the Israeli connection.

As things developed, it was Mangistu, not Sisai, who benefited politically from the creation of the Flame Division. It was he who appointed the division's commanders, thus ensuring their loyalty to his person. Mangistu was also careful to make sure that young members of the indoctrinated intelligentsia would not be recruited in significant numbers and that the majority of the new elite troops would be sons of peasants "who do not ask too many questions." At the same time, he was put in charge of the Derg's security and obtained control over a new 400-man unit that trained along with the Flame.[14] (Their commander, Lt. Col. Daniel Asfaw, was one of his closest associates.)

Unlike Mangistu, Sisai advocated that the army share power with leftist civilians in order to establish a "people's republic"—that is, he advocated a political solution to the Eritrean problem. Indeed, following publication of the Nine-Point Plan, the Derg appointed Sisai to head a committee to work for its implementation. When Mangistu and Atnafu's Peasants March failed, Sisai's prestige grew to such an extent as to give rise to speculation that he was about to depose them.[15] Apparently, he was working in this direction, in close cooperation with the commander of Ethiopian forces in Eritrea, the man responsible for the administration of martial law there, Brig. Gen. Getachaw Nadaw. The 42-year-old Eritrean-born soldier was appointed to this position in late January 1975, and after seeing the difficulties involved, he urged a political solution. Both Sisai and Getachaw, supported by some high-ranking officers, tried to establish contact with the leftist EPLF.[16] According to a publication of the EPLF Foreign Mission, Sisai, during his visit to Asmara in May 1976, had emphasized that Eritrea belonged to the Christian Marxists and not to the pro-Arab Muslims. It was also persistently rumored that Sisai and Getachaw were plotting to bring Eritrean-based forces to Addis Ababa to arrest Mangistu.

It was all over in early July 1976. On his return from an OAU conference abroad, Sisai was arrested, tried by the pro-Mangistu Derg, and promptly executed as a traitor. On that same day, 10 July 1976, Getachaw Nadaw was killed trying to resist arrest by the Derg's emissaries.[17]

The execution of Sisai Habte was an important event in the history of the Derg, but by this time the Derg (and the army it represented) was not the only source of power in the capital. The 1974 revolution had been conducted by two sectors: the military—led by junior officers and NCOs, who formed the Derg and seized power; and civilians—students, workers, intellectuals, and others who were instrumental in toppling the old order but lacked the cohesive leadership and power needed to become partners in the building of the new regime. It was only in mid-1975 that such leadership was provided following the return to Ethiopia of hundreds of exiles, the majority of whom were leftists and Marxists (many liberals left for Europe and America). The leftist-oriented, civilian sector eventually became a factor that competed for power with the Derg and aimed at the establishment of a people's republic. Two rival organizations were established. One, the Ethiopian People's Revolution Party (EPRP), perceived the Derg, especially as it was influenced by Mangistu, as a reactionary fascist junta.[18] It categorically rejected any cooperation with the regime and started a violent armed struggle in the capital and the provinces. The second movement, established in late 1975 and led by Dr. Hailu Fida and Dr. Nagade Gobaze, two French-educated intellectuals who had returned from exile following the deposition of the emperor, was called the All-Ethiopian Socialist Movement, better known by the acronym of its Amharic name, Mueson. The Mueson conceived the Derg as a necessary stage on the way to a future people's republic and therefore cooperated with it. Members of the Mueson were most influential in shaping the Derg's platform. In May 1976, they were given an active role when the Political Office of Mass Organizational Affairs (POMOA) was established to politicize the masses and train new cadres.

Both the EPRP and the Mueson advocated a political solution in Eritrea. As Marxists, they shared the belief that the conflict would be solved once a people's republic was established, and they clearly attached greater priority to advancing the revolution than to national unity. Furthermore, both movements were said to recognize Eritrea's right to self-determination and separatism.[19] Hailu Fida, the leader of the Mueson, saw the EPLF as a legitimate partner for negotiating a solution. His ideas were shared by the EPRP, which in March 1976 went so far as to issue a joint statement with the EPLF on the aims of the revolution.[20] The EPRP strongly criticized such actions as the Peasants March. The EPRP's military wing in the province of Tigre reportedly cooperated with the Eritrean organizations. Both organizations opposed Mangistu's policy of continuing the military dictatorship as well as his approach to the Eritrean issue.

While the Mueson cooperated with the Derg, in the second half of 1976 the EPRP launched a campaign of terrorism aimed at the assassination of Mangistu. EPRP murder squads proved most efficient in eliminating much of the leadership of the Mueson, but their attempts to assassinate Mangistu and his immediate followers were foiled by efficient squads of soldiers and organized civilians loyal to Mangistu. By late 1976, however, Mangistu seemed to be cornered. The military situation in Eritrea was deteriorating, the besieged army was demoralized, and Addis Ababa was a city of constant terrorism. In December, Mangistu's rivals in the Derg, headed by the Capt. Alamayhu Haile and Capt. Mogus Walda-Mikael, managed to persuade the council to reorganize itself, with the result that Mangistu's power (and Atnafu's) was diminished considerably.[21] The leftist captains (closely associates of the late Sisai Habte) were ready to cooperate with the EPRP in Addis Ababa and to work out a far-reaching compromise with the EPLF in Eritrea.[22]

On 3 February 1977, the cornered Mangistu made his move. After arresting his rivals with the help of his loyal guard, he managed to pass a vote in the Derg to execute them as traitors. Alamayhu and Mogus, as well as four of their associates, were promptly shot. A seventh victim of the firing squad was the Derg's chairman, Brig. Gen. Tafari Banti, who, though previously a hard-liner concerning Eritrea, was now ready to negotiate with the EPLF and was also collaborating with Mangistu's rivals.

Mangistu emerged from this bloodbath the undisputed chairman of the Derg. The vice-chairman, Lt. Col. Atnafu Abate, was still alive, but was cautious enough to keep a low profile. Mangistu could now try to implement his policy of "Unity or Death." The EPRP was systematically eliminated. The military option in Eritrea had to be solidly prepared, and the foundations of a new state machinery had to be laid. It was time to start mobilizing, arming, and training a massive peasant army and reorienting Ethiopia toward the Soviet Union.

The emergence of the Soviet Union as a main source of support and supplies for Ethiopia was a major achievement for Mangistu and his wing of the Derg. Their interest in Soviet arms was obvious. The United States had become a reluctant supplier, and its interests in the Red Sea seemed to be more compatible with those of the Saudis, the Egyptians, and the Sudanese. An Israeli effort to persuade Washington not to abandon Ethiopia proved futile. What was less obvious was the reason for the Soviet shift from its previous support for the Somalis and its indirect support for the Eritreans to an all-out orientation on Addis Ababa. The answer may be that in early 1977 the Soviets believed that they would not have to make such a choice. Indeed, it was quite apparent that the Soviets, underestimating the strength of local nationalisms, deceived themselves into believing that the conflicts in the Horn of Africa among their Marxist friends might be solved in the spirit of the Derg's National Democratic Revolution Program—namely, that the creation of a

Soviet Union of Ethiopia, in which the Eritreans and the Ogaden Somalis would enjoy local autonomy, might bring about a Pax Sovietica in the Horn. Thus, a region of growing strategic importance would become a zone of Soviet influence, and the Red Sea, an important link for the Western economies, would be at the Soviets' mercy.[23] In May 1977, Lt. Col. Mangistu Haila-Mariam, accompanied by his closest associates, was warmly received in Moscow,[24] where he succeeded in obtaining the weaponry formally promised in an agreement signed the previous December.

A month earlier, a huge effort to rebuild Ethiopia's armed forces had begun. On 12 April 1977, Mangistu delivered an emotion-laden speech over national radio and television in which he described the external threat to Ethiopia's integrity and announced a plan for a massive mobilization.[25]

A huge training camp had already been erected some 25 kilometers from Addis Ababa.[26] Here, among the tents and the huts of Camp Tatek ("Be Prepared"), Ethiopia was undergoing its most fundamental change since the deposition of Haile Selassie. Tens of thousands of peasants from all over the country, the majority from the southern provinces—many of them members of the provincial militia forces—assembled in Camp Tatek for intensive instruction by young army officers of proven loyalty to Mangistu. It was a revolutionary change—with a taste of a return to tradition, for Haile Selassie's modernization of the 1940s had meant the destruction of the provincial armies and the building of a professional army, Western-equipped and trained, of only 45,000 men. This time, Ethiopia's military potential was to be realized through the mobilization and training of provincial armies as part of one central militia. The Soviets provided the necessary arms, and Somali threats and humiliating defeats in Eritrea provided the patriotic motivation. At the same time, the professional standing army was reinforced, and by the end of 1977 the Ethiopian armed forces numbered some 100,000 regulars, 150,000 combat-ready militiamen, 400 Soviet-made tanks (T-65s and T-55s), 50–60 MiG-17s and MiG-21s (plus several U.S.-made F-5s), and thousands of artillery pieces and armored carriers. This force was far larger than all the other armies in the Horn combined.

The building of this huge army signaled the building of a new political establishment as well. Unlike in Eritrea, where the educated members of the local intelligentsia dominated the organizations and competed for power under the cloak of revolution, Ethiopia's new army was essentially a peasant army. It was apparent to those competing for leadership of the Derg that the key to power lay in the appointment of the commanders who would indoctrinate the trainees. As in the past, it was Mangistu who would emerge victorious in this power struggle.

Mangistu's rivals in the contest to shape the personal and ideological loyalty of the army were no longer his colleagues in the Derg, but the Mueson, which actively participated in recruitment through the Mueson-controlled POMOA.[27] Yet, from February 1977, following the purge of his rivals in the Derg, Mangistu undermined the position of Hailu Fida, Nagade Gobaze, and their associates in the POMOA and appointed his followers to various functions. By that time, he had already established a political movement of his own, Seded ("Fire of the Revolution"). When Camp Tatek was set up, the job of indoctrinating recruits was given exclusively to Seded. The Mueson tried to gain a foothold throughout May and June, but was forcefully prevented from doing so. Clashes between the two became increasingly frequent. There were, of course, some ideological differences between the movements, primarily over interpretation of the National Democratic Revolution Program. While the Mueson was ready to interpret the right to self-determination as implying the option of separatism, Seded favored regional self-administration under the slogan of "Unity or Death."[28] Despite the support of Soviet and Cuban advisers for Mueson, Mangistu succeeded in defeating the Mueson ideologists. In August, Hailu Fida and his associates fled to the countryside,[29] while Dr. Nagade Gobaze, who happened to be out of the country at the time, did not return. Others were arrested. Mangistu was the undisputed leader, and "Unity or Death" became the unchallenged official policy.

These developments in Ethiopia were carefully observed by the Eritreans, now increasingly successful in Eritrea and capturing its towns. But the writing was on the wall. During May and June some of the new Ethiopian units were sent to the north to accomplish whatever was possible before the beginning of the rains. Their performance was far from impressive, but it was enough to wipe out the military buffer created by the EDU, the TPLF, and the ALF—and it proved to be just a beginning. Then, when it seemed that Mangistu was about to move conclusively against the Eritreans, another regional development played into their hands: in July 1977 the Somalis started the Ogaden war.

Earlier, in March 1977, the idea of a Pax Sovietica in the region had suffered a severe blow. In Eritrea, the war had climaxed. Somali-Ethiopian tension culminated over the question of Djibouti, the territory of the Afar and the Issa, which the French were about to evacuate. The Somalis were quite vocal about re-emphasizing their nationalist claim to this main Ethiopian outlet to the sea. In the Ogaden Desert, which was claimed by the Somalis, the Somali-supported irredentist movement, the WSLF, became active. By that time the Soviets, still massively present in Somalia, had started arming the Ethiopians. President Fidel Castro of Cuba arrived in the region to try to work out a Marxist peace between President Siad Barre of Somalia and Chairman Mangistu. A secret meeting in neighboring Aden turned out to be a bitter disappointment for Castro. Siad and Mangistu both employed Marxism to underline their nationalist differences. Mangistu expressed his readiness to implement the National Democratic Revolution in the Somali-populated Ogaden, but only according to his interpretation of Ethiopian "Unity or Death." Siad remained committed to scientific-socialist fulfillment of Somali ethnic nationalism. He was, of course, halfway toward the Arab Red Sea camp, having discussed the matter with Numayri. From his point of view, he could hardly accept that his old Soviet supporters were supplying his Ethiopian enemy.

For Siad, the coming July was the decisive month. His planning staff advised him to use his army's superiority in Soviet-trained armor before the Ethiopians had time to digest the massive Soviet aid. Aided by the WSLF, the Somalis swept the desert, smashing the ill-equipped Ethiopian 3d Division and the ill-trained militias they encountered. By September the whole desert was in Somali hands, with the exception of two strategic towns, Harar and Dire-Dawa, which remained Ethiopian primarily due to the active participation of ten thousand Cuban troops in their defense. These two springboards back to the desert would be used by the Ethiopians (and Cubans) in the forthcoming February. By that time the balance of power would have changed totally, with the Somali army virtually destroyed. Two factors stopped the Ethiopians from punishing the Somalis on their own territory: the fear of U.S. involvement and the fact that Eritrea, and not the Ogaden, remained Ethiopia's main problem.

10. An Ethiopian Victory?

By the first half of 1978, virtually all of Eritrea was controlled by the Eritrean nationalists. The Eritrean capital, Asmara, though still held by the Ethiopian army, was under siege, its airport sporadically shelled by Eritrean mortars. The ELF-RC controlled the road to Tigre, and the EPLF the road to Massawa. In the town of Massawa itself, the Ethiopian army barely maintained its hold over the port and neighboring islands. It managed to withstand the assaults of the EPLF only because of help rendered by Soviet battleships. Of the remaining Eritrean towns, only Assab, Barentu, and Addi Qaih remained in Ethiopian hands.

Yet, it was quite clear to all concerned that sooner or later the pendulum would swing in the other direction. Ethiopia had managed to contain the Somalis and was about to smash their army, thanks to active Cuban support. The revamped Ethiopian army and militia force, their ranks increased, were being heavily armed by the Soviets and trained by the Cubans. The Somali invasion had played into the hands of hard-liner Mangistu, making his "Unity or Death" policy, at least for a while, a reality of life in the Ogaden.

In November 1977, Mangistu further strengthened his position in the Derg by eliminating the last of his opponents among the prominent members of the ruling body, Lt. Col. Atnafu Abate. Once again the dispute was purportedly over the Eritrean war, and once again the side advocating a political solution was defeated.

The real issue, however, was, as always, the competition for power and survival. In February 1977, following the executions of Mangistu's rivals in the Derg, Atnafu, till then careful not to provoke Mangistu, moved his residence to the Addis Ababa headquarters of the 4th Division, which was loyal to him. Since Mangistu enjoyed the support of the majority in the Derg as well as the Derg's battalion-size guard, Atnafu had to fortify his defenses.

During the next few months, Atnafu kept a low profile. Following the Somali invasion when all attention was focused on the Ogaden, he was put in charge of the Eritrean front. It was probably then that he started working independently of Mangistu, strengthening his position in both the 4th Division in Addis Ababa and the 2d Division in Eritrea. He tried to persuade his followers that because of Mangistu's policy the old army was losing ground politically to new Soviet-equipped and Cuban-trained units and to the militia. In the second week of October he clearly provoked Mangistu by conducting a highly publicized tour of the 2d Division. Despite his reputation as a hard-liner, Atnafu was now said to be seeking to promote a possible political solution in Eritrea. This was to be the cause of his downfall. Back in Addis Ababa he called on the Derg to adopt a more flexible policy, less dependent on the Soviets. Mangistu, himself under pressure from his younger, radical devotees (notably pro-Soviet 2d Lt. Lagase Asfaw), reacted by convincing the Derg that Atnafu was a traitor. Atnafu was promptly tried and executed (11 November 1977).

But Mangistu was still not in a position to exercise his military option in Eritrea. Fighting the Eritrean organizations in Eritrea was quite different from facing the Somalis in the Ogaden. The terrain in the northern province was such that quantitative superiority in troops and arms was not enough. After seventeen years of persistent fighting, the Eritreans were far better trained than the Somalis had been and were also more battle-experienced than the newly mobilized Ethiopian units. Above all, the Soviets and Cubans, whose planning and active participation had secured the military victory in the Ogaden, were reluctant to provide the same services in Eritrea. They also pressed for a political solution.

Indeed, an Eritrean war was a problem the Soviets wished to avoid. They had always considered the leftist-oriented Eritrean organizations an asset. In aiding the Eritreans mostly through radical Arabs, Moscow had, so to speak, rocked the cradle of Eritreanism. The ideal solution from the Soviet point of view would have been the implementation of the National Democratic Revolution, modified in a way that would permit Eritrea to be an entity federated with Ethiopia enjoying internal political, cultural, and administrative autonomy. Such a solution had to be achieved by political means and not—as Mangistu wanted—by destroying the Eritrean organizations. The Soviets would have preferred to see an "Ethiopian Soviet Union" established in the Horn of Africa, which they hoped would be ruled by an ideologically committed communist party and not by a group of army officers. Accordingly, they hoped that the various autonomous units would be controlled by local party branches. According to this conception, Eritrea would remain intact as one of several autonomous units. The radical leaders of Eritrean organizations would form a branch of the Ethiopian Communist Party or, preferably, would establish an Eritrean Communist Party. A similar solution applied over the Ogaden would pave the way for the Soviets to return to Mogadishu. Such a regional federation, which would be joined enthusiastically by the PDRY as well, would be of enormous strategic value for the Soviets. Crushing the Eritreans in the interest of a strong Ethiopian regime centered on Addis Ababa could hardly serve their long-term interests in the region in the same way.

Fighting the Eritreans was even more problematic for the Cubans. In early 1978 Cuban brigades, estimated in April 1978 at 17,000 men, constituted the Ethiopians' main professional striking force. As the fighting in the Ogaden had demonstrated, the new Ethiopian army was still incapable of conducting the sophisticated operations required to recapture occupied towns without massive support from the Cuban units. Yet the Cubans were even more reluctant than the Soviets to repeat the Ogaden story in Eritrea. Their relationships with the Eritrean leaders and organizations had been closer and warmer. Moreover, in general the Cubans—always at the service of the Soviets—had made great efforts to project an image of being persistent supporters of liberation movements. President Castro had invested a great deal over the years in becoming a prominent leader of the Third World. Direct assistance to the destruction of what was widely recognized by the more vocal leaders of the Third World as a progressive liberation movement was something Castro could hardly afford. Thus, supporting Mangistu became problematic for the Soviets and the Cubans if the Ethiopian effort was to be diverted from repulsing the invading Somalis to crushing the Eritreans.

Undaunted, Mangistu was determined to do just that. But since the Soviets and Cubans restricted their assistance to general planning, advice, and logistics, Ethiopian efforts in February and March 1978 to relieve the pressure on the Eritrean-besieged Asmara and Massawa were doomed to failure.

Between 3 and 5 April 1978, Mangistu paid a secret visit to Moscow to discuss the Eritrean issue with President Brezhnev and Prime Minister Kosygin. Apparently nothing of substance was achieved there; in any case the Cubans, who had to do the actual fighting, stuck to their own opinion. During the third week of April, Mangistu went to see Castro in Havana. Although the Cubans gave Mangistu a hero's welcome, they were unyielding in their refusal to render him assistance in Eritrea by active participation in combat. Castro urged a political solution. He seems to have preferred a solution based on political, administrative, and cultural autonomy for Eritrea within the Ethiopian state, and he wanted this achieved *before* the destruction of the Eritrean organizations. Mangistu returned to Addis Ababa empty-handed with the rainy season only six weeks away.

Back in Ethiopia, Mangistu intensified military preparations in Eritrea. The victory over the Somalis was completed by late February, and the Ethiopian military effort shifted northward. By late April, some 100,000 combat-ready militia and army regulars were assembled along the Eritrean border (mainly in camps near Addigrat, Makalle, Adwa, and Humera) and in the besieged Asmara. The Ras Alula airfield at Makalle was expanded with the help of the Cubans, and hundreds of air raids were conducted from there against the Eritreans throughout May. Mangistu himself went there to inspect and encourage his troops. Sporadic battles and probing attacks were launched, and there were repeated attempts to break the siege of the Eritrean capital. However, this was still far from being a concentrated military effort; the chairman of the Derg was presumably still hoping to persuade the Cubans and Soviets to help him solve the Eritrean problem his way.

The Cubans and Soviets had other ideas. They strongly opposed Mangistu's solution and pushed instead for a negotiated settlement; ignoring Mangistu's pressures, they explored the possibility of promoting his opponents in the capital, such as the Marxist-oriented Mueson, which also supported negotiations with the Eritrean organizations. Moreover, if they came to power, these ideologically committed leftist civilians would assure the future of Soviet and Cuban influence in Ethiopia.

Thus, while Mangistu was trying to promote war against the Eritreans, the Cubans, with the help of South Yemen, were helping the members of the Mueson who were trying to revive their movement through the formation of a workers' party in Addis Ababa. In the first week of May 1978, the Cubans succeeded in smuggling into Addis Ababa from Europe Dr. Nagade Gobaze, a prominent leader of the movement who had escaped arrest by Mangistu earlier in 1977. He tried to pull strings from the Cuban Embassy, contacting trade unionists and leftist Derg members. Mangistu discovered this attempt, and both Nagade and the Cuban ambassador were forced to leave the country on 14 May 1978.

The battles in Eritrea throughout late May and the first half of June were just a warm-up. The major offensive that observers expected to be launched from Tigre and Bagemdir was delayed, apparently because Mangistu still hoped to convince the Cubans to participate more actively. Meanwhile, the Eritreans now seemed inclined to consider a political settlement. In early June, the ELF-RC's Ahmad Nasir left secretly for Moscow. Later in the same month, he and the EPLF's Ramadan Nur made a public offer of direct negotiations with the Derg under Soviet auspices. They again rejected the Nine-Point Plan and the National Democratic Revolution Program and emphasized that recognition of the right to self-determination should be the basis of negotiations.

The Derg was under pressure from Cuba, the Soviet Union, South Yemen, Libya, and others, including some of its own members, to try negotiations. In response to these pressures, the Derg organized a seminar in Addis Ababa that was the first public debate ever conducted in Ethiopia on the Eritrean issue. For ten consecutive days beginning 16 June 1978, no less than 900 delegates—including virtually all 80 Derg members, government ministers, trade union leaders, and almost all foreign-based senior diplomats—assembled in the capital's city hall. Hundreds of speeches were made, and the highly publicized event turned out to be the final showdown in the long competition between those favoring a military solution and those urging negotiations. As the marathon seminar progressed, the discussion was channeled into consensus: using Marxist vocabulary, panelist after panelist outlined "genuine efforts" to reach a peaceful solution in Eritrea in the past and their frustration by the "treacherous bandits" who were demanding nothing less than full independence. Mangistu's presence in the seminar was undoubtedly an important factor in the creation of such a consensus. In answer to questions put to him by participants, he said that "the reactionary war in Eritrea is substantially the same as that of the Ogaden." He claimed that "reactionary Arab states were seeking to set up a puppet state in Eritrea and attack Ethiopia from this base." One of Mangistu's associates, Lt. Col. Berhanu Bayeh, concluded that "there was no alternative to dealing a decisive blow to the confirmed archreactionary separatists and liberating the oppressed masses of the region." Lieutenant Tamrat, in charge of information and public relations for the Derg, summarized and concluded the seminar by saying that Ethiopian struggles against the Eritrean secessionists "must be fought to the last man."[1]

Immediately after, the Ethiopian army camping in Tigre and Bagemdir crossed into Eritrea. The Soviets and Cubans confined their participation to planning and to giving close advice at the brigade level.

The rest of the events in Eritrea in 1978 may be told as pure military history. Even without direct Cuban participation in combat, and in spite of the rains, the Ethiopian reoccupation of Eritrea was fast and sure:

23 July 1978. Tessenei becomes the first town to be retaken (from ELF-RC).

27 July 1978. Addi Ugri recaptured; Massawa fully reoccupied.

28 July 1978. EPLF announces a tactical withdrawal.

30 July 1978. Decamere falls.

Early August 1978. Only Agordat remains in ELF-RC hands; Saganaiti and Digsa fall; Barentu's siege broken.

9 August 1978. Agordat captured by the Ethiopians; EPLF evacuates all urban centers and major villages to concentrate on the defense of Keren.

27 November 1978. After long, bitter, and costly battles, Keren falls to the Ethiopian army.

The fall of Keren and the Ethiopian reoccupation of all urban centers in Eritrea signified a fundamental change in the military balance. The Eritrean organizations were not destroyed, but their chances of defeating the Ethiopian armed forces and recapturing Eritrea became remote. What had seemed just a year earlier a feasible military option for fulfilling Eritrean nationalism was rendered impossible and seems likely to remain so for the foreseeable future.

Meanwhile, the regional political system of the Red Sea continued to develop in the pattern discernible since the middle of 1977, with the major local powers growing increasingly hostile to the idea of an independent Eritrea. Eritrean leaders—primarily those of the stronger movement, the EPLF—made it quite clear to all concerned that an independent Eritrea would become another South Yemen, radiating radicalism and fomenting regional instability. In Riyadh, where the existence of South Yemen caused much anxiety, an Eritrean state was seen as a nightmare. A Soviet-Cuban presence was bad enough, but penetration may be a passing phenomenon: a state, once established and legitimized, remains forever.

Egypt, too, has in the meantime reoriented its regional policy. In November 1977 President Sadat visited Jerusalem; in September 1978 Egypt and Israel signed the Camp David agreement, and in March 1979 a peace treaty was signed between Cairo and Jerusalem. The implications of this change for the Middle East and the Horn of Africa remain to be seen. Two short-run implications may nevertheless be discussed. First, the Israeli-Egyptian rapprochement (and later the revolution in Iran) has diverted global and Middle Eastern attention away from the Red Sea and the Horn of Africa. The Eritreans missed the opportunity to capitalize politically and militarily on the attention they received in 1977, and it is highly unlikely that the opportunity will repeat itself. Second, Sadat's initiative brought relations between Egypt on the one hand and Syria, Iraq, and the PLO on the other to the point of active hostility. From the Egyptians' point of view, the ELF-RC was identified with Syria and Iraq, and the EPLF with the PLO. An independent Eritrea led by one or both of these organizations would be no less a nightmare for them than it would be for the Saudis. It is almost unthinkable that Egypt, unless it once again finds itself in the throes of Nasserist Pan-Arabism, would be interested in the establishment of an Aden-type Eritrea.

Sadat's initiative further strengthened Egyptian-Sudanese relations. President Numayri was among the few Arabs who supported the daring Egyptian move. From the perspective of 1979, Egyptian-Sudanese relations may solidify as Egypt grows increasingly disappointed at the Arab reaction to its new orientation. Furthermore, the more Egyptian public opinion favors Egyptianism at the expense of Arabism, the more Egypt will turn its attention to the Nile Valley. It is worth remembering in this context that prior to 1954, before President Nasser initiated the departure from Egyptian nationalism into messianic Arabism, Egyptian nationalists saw the Sudan as an integral part of Egypt. No one can tell what renewed Egyptian interest in the Sudan would mean politically. Chances are, however, that an Egyptian-Sudanese alliance would contribute to regional stability and to a growing tendency to solve local problems through political means.

It seems that the Eritrean movement, at least as long as it is under its present leadership, can do very little to mobilize substantial regional support. From this point of view, the best it can hope for is to receive sufficient aid from its old Middle Eastern allies (Syria, Iraq, and the PLO) to allow it to conduct a prolonged guerrilla war. (Even this has become problematic, since the erstwhile supporters of Eritrean nationalism are also allied with the Soviet Union. The PLO, for example—as always in the service of Moscow—started a diplomatic campaign in early 1978 to persuade both the EPLF and the ELF-RC to accept the idea of Eritrean autonomy under Ethiopian sovereignty.)

Ethiopia faces enormous problems. The regime suffers from the destruction of the middle class and a shattered economy, and has still to cope seriously with the challenge of internal diversity. Yet the general trend is toward solidification of a renewed centralism. It is therefore quite probable that the regional powers—Saudi Arabia, Egypt, the Sudan, and Israel—each in its own turn and out of a mutual interest in promoting stability and preserving the status quo, will come to terms with Addis Ababa.

The key question, however, remains the future of relations between Ethiopia and the Soviet Union. Does it make sense to anticipate an eventual crisis in these relations? Judging from history, such a crisis is very probable. Two main themes in Ethiopia's history seem to be relevant. First, as already discussed, Ethiopia was seldom defeated by other civilizations, including late nineteenth century European imperialism. Having succeeded in maintaining political independence for centuries, the Ethiopians have developed nationalist pride, a deep sense of self-respect, and a well-proven and tested ability to neutralize those foreigners who have tried to patronize them. The old imperialist powers all learned this in their time, and Westerners who have dealt with independent Ethiopians have had to follow the same rules. Those who accepted that the Ethiopians were their own masters managed to establish fruitful relations; those who did not were promptly shown the way out. Are the Soviets, who recently failed so dramatically in their concourse with nations such as Egypt, the Sudan, and Somalia that had lived for almost a century under European imperialism, capable of passing the Ethiopian test? And if so, for how long?

One important chapter in Ethiopia's history is worth remembering in this context—the time when the Ethiopian state was destroyed by foreign invaders. During the years 1529–1542, the Somali and Afar Muslims, united under the leadership of Imam Ahmad ben Ibrahim, managed to defeat and shatter the Christian Ethiopian empire. Like the mid-1970s, this was a period during which the Red Sea was of great strategic importance, and the Ottomans and the Portuguese competed for control of the sea routes to India. Then as now, mighty foreigners came to the rescue of Ethiopia. In 1541, some four hundred Portuguese soldiers joined the emperor, helped him to regroup and train his followers, and participated in active combat. The next year, Imam Ahmad was killed, and the Somalis and Afar Muslims went back to their coast. Ethiopia was saved. Following this, close relations were established between Ethiopia and the European Catholic church. Many missionaries and church officials capitalized on this; they established themselves in Ethiopia's main religious centers and started interfering with Ethiopian affairs. This process ended dramatically some eight decades later with popular unrest resulting in the Catholics' expulsion. In the ensuing centuries, while Protestant missionaries were generally tolerated in Ethiopia, their Catholic colleagues were often maltreated. Have the Soviets bothered to study such chapters in history?

No doubt, the Soviets have learned much from their ouster in other Oriental and African states and will try to avoid past pitfalls so as to maintain a position in Ethiopia. Or, has Ethiopia's adoption of Marxism muted some of the traditional Ethiopian reluctance to cooperate with an outside power? Only time can provide an answer. But another factor seems to tilt a balanced appraisal toward a possible falling out of the two states.

Another major theme of Ethiopia's past, which also stemmed from its long, isolated independence, was the dominance among Ethiopians of a world-view centered on Ethiopia. Generally speaking, unlike some neighboring civilizations, the Ethiopians failed to develop ideologies that encouraged active interest in the world around them. The universal values and notions that Islam and later Arab nationalism provided to their Middle Eastern and North African adherents—or the sense of affiliation to large empires that other Africans, willingly or not, had to develop in modern times—remained essentially alien to the Ethiopians. Though possible, it is highly improbable that the Ethiopians will act in the service of non-Ethiopian interests outside the boundaries of their country. Will the Soviets compromise with that? Have they invested so much just to help Ethiopia maintain its territorial integrity? Would they refrain from pressing a strong Ethiopia in the future to act in the service of Soviet strategy, mistakenly conceiving Ethiopia as another Nasserist Egypt or Castroite Cuba?

The Soviet Union, of course, could be content to use Ethiopian land and sea bases for decades before pressing Ethiopian forces into regional or world arenas. After all, this was the course of events that developed between Moscow and Cuba, which saw its international revolutionary duty in Africa fifteen years after Castro came to power in the Caribbean island.

Nothing is potentially detrimental to future Ethiopian-Soviet relations. Despite conflicting strategic interests and Ethiopia's vital need for Western economic investments and aid, a long Soviet stay cannot be excluded. First, as we have seen, major political decisions in revolutionary Ethiopia were made in a context of violent political competition and at the very personal risk of the initiator. This is still the name of the game in the Derg's palace, and some contenders to the chairmanship are allied with Soviet and East German advisers in charge of security. At present, if Mangistu decided to oust the Soviets, he could not avoid a reopening of internal political competition, of which he might himself fall victim. Second—and this relates to one of my main conclusions—the Eritrean movement is still a threat to Ethiopia. As a guerrilla force, it is very much alive and waiting for a major power to turn it again from a nuisance force into the embryo of a future state. So far the Soviets have done little to prevent the Eritreans from playing such a future role. By not helping Mangistu crush the Eritrean organizations, the Soviets hold a stick over the Derg's head to ensure its good behavior.

From the perspective of late 1981, the assumption that the struggle was resolved in 1978 remains valid. The main processes in the two struggling camps continued to develop along the lines described above. Ethiopia has become increasingly centralized, while the Eritrean movement, militarily on the defensive, has become increasingly fragmented. Politically, the last few years have seen a stalemate in the struggle between the camps, and a series of repetitive guerrilla actions can hardly be expected to change the basic fact that emerges from the analysis of the previous pages: the Eritreans missed their historic opportunity to fulfill their nationalist aspirations.

The story of the struggle over Eritrea is yet another proof of two universal truths. One is that the use of force to quell a people's aspirations is often counterproductive; indeed, the Ethiopian army may be considered a major factor in the creation of Eritrean nationalism. The other is that the dogmatic pursuit of ideologies and personal ambitions is equally counterproductive. It is because they were prisoners of such an approach that Eritrean leaders failed in their endeavor: the local and regional reality of the 1975–1977 period was clearly favorable to them, but blinkered by irrelevant dogmas and personal ambitions, they failed to perceive this. The Ethiopians, with lesser ideological commitments, were able to shape reality to their will.

At the same time, the story of the Eritrean conflict has been a contemporary replay of a local historical theme. As on many occasions in the past, while the inhabitants of the Ethiopian heartland became militarily united under an ambitious autocrat in the face of challenge, the inhabitants of the peripheral coastal areas fell victim to disunity and decentralist tendencies resulting in military and political weakness.

Is the Ethiopian victory final? In answer to this question, it currently seems possible to prophesize only in a negative way: Eritrean victory may realistically be excluded as a future possibility. The chances of those identified with Eritrean nationalism achieving it by military victory over the Ethiopian armed forces seems very remote. At the same time, Eritreanism as a nationalist sense of affiliation, and more so as a strong negation of Ethiopianism, seems strong enough to ensure its continued existence and to provide the motivation for a long, guerrilla war. It is equally improbable that the Ethiopians will manage to cope with such a war militarily and to destroy the Eritrean organizations on the battlefield.

To achieve real victory over the separatists, the Ethiopians have to abandon the belief that they can achieve this through violence. On the contrary, the lesson they have to learn from the history of the conflict is that it was mainly due to use of such methods that an Eritrean nationalist movement emerged out of what had initially, in the early 1950s, been little more than a problem of Islamic-inspired local separatism. Indeed, the emergence of such a nationalist movement was otherwise against all odds. Eritrea is not a natural unit. There is nothing about the area that causes the forces within it to coalesce. On the contrary, all the forces around Eritrea tend to exercise a stronger force on the area than any counterforces within it—Ethiopia's Christianity and Tigrean traditions attract the Christian-Tigrean population, while the traditions of neighboring Muslim and Arab communities or various tribal traditions affect the various elements in the Muslim population. What nationalism there is in Eritrea is dependent largely on the emotions and ambitions of the younger members of the intelligentsia. It is to the tragedy of all parties concerned that this generation was shaped during a period in which Ethiopianism was almost always identified with deprivation. A constructive solution, from an Ethiopian point of view, may therefore be achieved only after a long period of careful political, administrative, economic, and social approaches by Addis Ababa to the problems of Eritreans. That may achieve a victory for Ethiopianism. Unfortunately, after some three decades in which the Ethiopians made almost every possible mistake in Eritrea, it would seem unrealistic to expect that such a policy will bear fruit in the future.

On paper, the National Democratic Revolutionary Program makes sense as a framework for such an approach. The Eritreans, like other Ethiopians, would enjoy autonomy in the spheres of culture and self-administration while belonging to an economic and political system centered on Addis Ababa. The main weakness of the program is that it implies that Eritrea, an entity that in the ninety years of its existence has played a pivotal role in the history of the whole region, will have to be erased from the map. Is this realistic?

Appendixes

1. Eritrean Organizations, 1962–1978

1964–1968: Supreme Council and Revolutionary Command based in Sudan. Fighters organized in regional commands (*willayas*).

August 1968: The three commands of eastern Eritrea unite to form the Tripartite Union and develop contacts with such exiles as Uthman Sabi and Walda-Ab.

August 1969: The fighters in the field form the General Command and break with the exiles of the Supreme Council.

June 1970: Uthman Sabi, Walda-Ab, and their fellow exiles join with members of the Tripartite Union to form the People's Liberation Front (PLF). The Christian members of the former Tripartite Union form other groups.

December 1971: Members of the western regional command reunite with exiles headed by Idris Adam and form the Eritrean Liberation Front–Revolutionary Council (ELF-RC).

February 1972: Formation of Eritrean People's Liberation Front (EPLF), with its leadership abroad known as the Foreign Mission (FM).

1972–1974: The ELF-RC refuses to recognize the EPLF. Continuous war between the two claims over a thousand dead.

Late 1974: Following the Ethiopian revolution, both organizations grow. The majority of the new recruits are Christian Tigreans. War between the two organizations ends, and there is even some military cooperation between them.

Early 1975: Influence of young cadres in both organizations grows, leading to splits with exiles. Trend to the left and at the expense of Arabism.

May 1975: Fighters establish new ELF-RC.

September 1975: ELF-RC maintains "Unity Before Victory." Forms union with FM, later to discover that it no longer represents EPLF.

March 1976: Formal rupture of relations between EPLF and FM. Wild accusations on both sides.

July 1976: ELF-RC recognizes FM as a third Eritrean nationalist organization.

January 1977: EPLF congress. Formal adoption of "Revolution Before Unity" policy. Partial cooperation with ELF-RC expressed in establishment of joint front. FM rejected totally.

April 1977: FM, having mobilized fighters, renamed ELF-PLF.

January 1977–early 1978: EPLF and ELF-RC succeed in gaining control of Eritrean towns. EPLF proves more efficient and stronger.

June 1977: ELF-RC and EPLF establish a coordinating body, the National Democratic Front (NDF) to include non-Eritrean anti-Derg organizations, but not the ELF-PLF. Meanwhile, Saudi money and Sudanese aid channeled to the ELF-PLF.

July 1977: The conquest of Keren by the EPLF shows that the NDF was a fiction from the start. The ELF-RC recognizes the ELF-PLF as entitled to membership in the NDF. Close military cooperation between them.

July–August 1977: Internal clashes in ELF-RC over policy on EPLF and ELF-PLF deserters. Formation of new factions in the ELF-RC, internal instability in the EPLF. The ELF-RC accuses the EPLF of betraying Eritreanism and collaborating with Ethiopians and Soviets.

August–October 1977: The ELF-RC and the EPLF negotiate.

October 1977: NDF reactivated; ELF-PLF denied recognition.

November–December 1977: Mutual recriminations by leaders of all organizations. Fears of another fratricidal war. Although both organizations besiege Asmara, they fail to make a combined effort to take it.

Early 1978: Ethiopia's new army aided by Cubans and Soviets regains superiority in Eritrea.

2. The Government of Ethiopia and the Eritrean Question, 1962–1978

1962–1970: Eritrea's Governor-general Asrate, head of the political faction known as the Shoan nobility group, tries to make Eritrea his power base in the struggle tor power against Prime Minister Aklilu, who heads a rival group composed largely of ministers and generals. Rivalry encouraged by emperor, so no coordinated Ethiopian effort in Eritrea. Asrate's political orientation on Christian Eritreans, Aklilu's on the army.

1970–1974: Aklilu's victory over Asrate leads to military government in Eritrea, although new military governor also a member of the Shoan group. The army's tough and brutal measures alienate Christians, while the Eritrean-recruited police and commandos are pushed aside. Growing resentment in army due to social and ideological gap between members and commanders of companies (the operative military unit) and their superior officers.

February–June 1974: Protest movement in the army, formation of committees in the various battalions, and civil unrest result in the fall of Aklilu's government. The emperor isolated, but the Shoan nobility group manages temporarily to exploit the situation and seize power. The units deployed in Eritrea play an important role in the change. Stalemate in Eritrea.

Late June 1974–12 September 1974: The protest movement develops into a revolution with the establishment of the Derg, a collegial military council made up of representatives of battalion committees. No member has stronger power than his colleagues. Haile Selassie deposed (12 September). Members of the Shoan nobility arrested (executed, together with Aklilu's group and others, on 23 November 1974); Lt. Gen. Aman Andom becomes chairman of the Derg. Wave of terrorism started by Eritrean separatists, meets with violent army retaliation.

August–November 1974: Chairman Aman attempts to achieve a political solution in Eritrea, with or without EPLF. Major Mangistu gaining influence in the still collegial Derg. Manages to appoint his associate, hard-liner Brig. Gen. Tafari Banti, as commander of the armed forces in Eritrea. Both call for military action. Aman fails to persuade Eritreans to accept political solution, and Mangistu persuades Derg to send a brigade from 1st Division (supporters of Aman) to Eritrea. Aman killed resisting arrest on 23 November 1974. Tafari Banti replaces Aman as chairman of Derg.

1975–February 1977: Mangistu works for a military solution together with Lt. Col. Atnafu. Builds his position on the slogan "Unity or Death" and enjoys support of majority of NCOs in Derg, but opposed by Marxists inside and outside the Derg, who call for revolution as precondition to unity and propose a political solution in Eritrea based on the National Democratic Revolution Program. In early February 1977 Mangistu manages to eliminate this opposition, including his former associate Tafari.

1977–   : Mangistu rebuilds army and state machinery. Undisputed leader of the Derg. Soviets and Cubans help to build a new army; rebuff Somali invasion. New army to try to fulfill Mangistu's slogan, "Unity or Death."

Abbreviations Used in Notes

AC	*Africa Confidential*
CSM	*Christian Science Monitor*
EC	Ethiopian calendar
EH	*Ethiopian Herald*
FT	*Financial Times*
IHT	*International Herald Tribune*
JP	*Jerusalem Post*
NYT	*New York Times*
WP	*Washington Post*

Notes

Chapter 1

1. Detailed studies on the structure and organization of Eritrean society may be found in Carlo Conti Rossini, *Principi di Diritto Conseutudinario dell'Eritrea* (Rome: Tipografia dell'Unione Editrice, 1916); Ruffillo Perini, *Di Qua Dal Mareb* (Florence: Tipografia Cooperativa, 1905); S. F. Nadel, "Land Tenure of the Eritrean Plateau," *Africa* (London) 16 (1946): 1–22, 99–109; Zawde Gabra-Sellasse [Zewde Gabre-Selassie], "Eritrea and Ethiopia in the Context of the Red Sea and Africa" (Washington, D.C.: Woodrow Wilson International Center, unpublished ms., 1976); John Spencer Trimingham, *Islam in Ethiopia* (London: Oxford University Press, 1962); Stephen Hemsley Longrigg, *A Short History of Ethiopia* (Oxford: Clarendon Press, 1945); and Great Britain, War Office, "Military Report on Eritrea" (London: Public Record Office, PRO, WO 33/410, n.d. [1909?]).

2. For a detailed bibliography on Eritrea, see Kassahun Checole, "Eritrea: A Preliminary Bibliography," *Africana Journal* 6 (1975): 303–14. For the Italian period, consult, among others, Longrigg, *Short History of Eritrea*; Margery Perham, *The Government of Ethiopia*, 2d ed. (Evanston, Ill.: Northwestern University Press, 1969); Y. Gershoni, "The Relationship Between Italy-Eritrea-Ethiopia in the Years 1896–1935" (Tel Aviv: Tel Aviv University, M.A. thesis, 1976); and Gabra-Sellasse, "Eritrea and Ethiopia."

3. Later these families regained some of their importance as the British (1941–1952) and Haile Selassie took them into their administrations.

4. For Eritrea under the British, consult Gerald Kennedy Nicholas Trevaskis, *Eritrea: A Colony in Transition, 1941–1952* (London: Oxford University Press, 1960); D. C. Cumming, "The Disposal of Eritrea," *Middle East Journal* 7, no. 1 (Winter 1953): 18–32; and Estelle Sylvia Pankhurst and Richard Pankhurst, *Ethiopia and Eritrea: The Last Phase of the Reunion Struggle, 1941–1952* (Woodford Green, Eng.: Lalibela House, 1953).

5. For relevant British correspondence from Eritrea, consult the Public Record Office's War Office files, especially nos. 168, 219–21, and 255. For details, see Haggai Erlich, "'Tigrean Nationalism,' British Involvement and Haile-Sellasse's Emerging Absolutism: Northern Ethiopia, 1941–1943," *Asian and African Studies* (Jerusalem and Haifa) 15, no. 1 (1982).

6. See Lloyd Ellingson, "The Emergence of Political Parties in Eritrea, 1941–1950," *Journal of African History* 18 (1977): 261–81.

7. For details, consult Trevaskis, *Eritrea*; Gabra-Sellasse, "Eritrea and Ethiopia"; and Pankhurst and Pankhurst, *Ethiopia and Eritrea*.

8. For the federation period, see Gabra-Sellasse, "Eritrea and Ethiopia"; Lloyd Ellingson, "The Origins and Development of the Eritrean Liberation Movement," in Robert L. Hess, ed., *Proceedings of the Fifth International Conference on Ethiopian Studies* (Chicago, 1978, session B); Ernest W. Luther, *Ethiopia Today* (Stanford: Stanford University Press, 1958); and Haggai Erlich, "The Eritrean Autonomy, 1952–1962: Its Failure and Contribution to Further Escalation," in Yoram Dinstein, ed., *Models of Autonomy* (New Brunswick, N.J.: Rutgers University Press, 1981), pp. 171–82.

9. For the Eritrean constitution and relevant legal discussions, consult United Nations, General Assembly, *Official Records, 7th Session: Supplement no. 15* (1952), pp. 76–89; Arthur A. Schiller, "Eritrea: Constitution and Federation with Ethiopia," *American Journal of Comparative Law* 2 (1953): 375–83; and Eritrean Liberation Front, *The Federal Case of Eritrea with Ethiopia* (Damascus, n.d.).

10. For full text, see Perham, *Government of Ethiopia*, p. 433.

11. A detailed description of the methods applied to Eritrean Christians who opposed reunification can be found in a long confession by an ex-member of both the EPLF and the ELF-RC, Haile Walda-Sellasse. His story, entitled "Man yemasker yanabara—man yarda yaqabara," was published in nine installments in the Ethiopian Amharic daily *Addis Zaman* (Addis Ababa), 24 Maskaram 1972–3 Teqemt 1972 Ethiopian calendar (EC; 4–14 October 1979).

12. Luther, *Ethiopia Today*, p. 147.

13. Uthman Salih Sabi [Othman Saleh Sabi], *The History of Eritrea*, trans. by Muhammad Fawaz al-Azem (Beirut, n.d. [1974]), p. 249. According to Uthman, the Eritrean Liberation Movement was established in 1958 in Port Sudan.

14. Striking examples of this can be found in ibid. and Eritrean People's Liberation Front, *In Defense of the Eritrean Revolution* (New York, 1978). Most pieces written by Eritreans tend to show this bias.

15. See Longrigg, *Short History of Eritrea*; and Tadesse Tamrat, *Church and State in Ethiopia, 1270–1527* (London: Oxford University Press, 1972).

16. See Haggai Erlich, *Ethiopia and Eritrea During the Scramble for Africa: A Political Biography of Ras Alula* (Tel Aviv: Tel Aviv University, Shiloah Center; East Lansing: Michigan State University Press, 1982).

Chapter 2

1. See "Letter from Eritrea," *Africa* 4, no. 22 (8 November 1963); *Africa* 7, no. 9 (6 May 1966); and *Domenica del Corriere* (Milan), 6 April 1971.

2. Interview with Idris Adam in *Tricontinental*, 1968, pp. 56–70; and Richard Loban, "The Eritrean War: Issues and Implications," *Canadian Journal of*

African Studies 10 (1976): 355–46. According to *Africa Confidential* (*AC*; London), 27 November 1970, the Supreme Council had only seven members.

3. See the article by an ELF fighter in *Ethiopian Herald* (*EH*; Addis Ababa), 24 September 1967.

4. Till the mid-1960s, the Ethiopian government apparently enjoyed the support of the majority of the Christian highlanders. See, for example, Anthony Vigo, "Between Two Worlds," *Africa Today* (New York), October 1965, pp. 6–8; Vigo, an American student, spent the period 1962–1964 in the village of Ad Teclesan, which later became an EPLF center. For Christian support for the separatists, see *Paese Sera* (Rome), 9 May 1967, for a description by the first European journalist to visit the ELF camps, Franco Prattico, "Viaggio nell'Eritrea in Fiamme" (issued also in Arabic by the ELF: *Rihla ila Irtriya al-mulhaba*, Damascus, n.d.); *Washington Post* (*WP*), 30 April 1967; and *EH*, 10 November 1967.

5. *Africa* 7, no. 9 (6 May 1966); *New York Times* (*NYT*), 30 April 1967; A. Dumuro, *Gazette de Lausanne*, 7 March 1967; and Patrick Gilkes, *The Dying Lion* (New York: St. Martin's Press, 1975), p. 197.

6. EPLF, *Taqrir siyyasi an al-azma fi harakat tahrir Irtriya wata 'sis quwat al-tahrir al-sha' biyya* [A political report on the crisis of the Eritrean Liberation Front and the establishment of the popular liberation forces—hereafter cited as "A Political Report"] (Beirut, n.d. [1971?]). See also Zawde Gabra-Sellasse [Zewde Gabre-Selassie], "Eritrea and Ethiopia in the Context of the Red Sea and Africa" (Washington, D.C.: Woodrow Wilson International Center, unpublished ms., 1976), p. 110; *EH*, 10 November 1967; *AC*, 27 November 1970; Radio Damascus, 18 January 1968, in *BBC/ME*, 20 January 1968; and *Eritrea: New Bulletin* (Damascus), December 1967 and January 1968.

7. According to Walda-Ab Walda-Mariam, "An Open Letter to Brothers Idris Muhammad Adam, Taha Nur, Idris Qladyus, Sayyid Muhammad, and Muhammad Salih" (in Arabic), Cairo, 8 March 1969, 5 pp.

8. "A Political Report."

9. The closing of the Suez Canal as a result of the 1967 war had a devastating effect on Eritrea. Eritrea was at the time poised to experience a significant jump in economic prosperity because investment in the food industry (winter fruits and vegetables, meat and dairy products, food processing) had placed it in a position to enter the European market with reasonable chances of success. Everything depended on efficient transportation through the Suez Canal. When the canal was closed and remained closed until 1975, much of the investment—made by the Ethiopian government as well as by Italians and other foreigners, including Israelis to a modest extent—did not produce dividends. Job markets that should have expanded failed to do so. Some winter fruits and vegetables were exported by air during the late 1960s and early 1970s, but this was a marginal activity. Some trade was developed with Arab countries, providing them with products such as cookies, candy, cheese, sausage, and wine, but a real takeoff did not occur. By the time the canal reopened, political confusion in Ethiopia had set in. The social and political significance of the Suez closing was a direct result of the economic downturn—or the failure to achieve an economic upturn—that resulted. Large numbers of young people failed to find work and, worse still, became depressed

and frustrated. Some opportunities for work abroad developed during this period. Some Eritreans found jobs across the Red Sea in Arab countries. Some were brought to Israel to work, and some went to Italy. Others went to other parts of Ethiopia, which were less directly affected by the Suez cutoff, although it had a debilitating effect on the economy as a whole.

10. *AC*, 13 March 1970; "A Political Report"; and Radio Addis Ababa, 30 May and 26 September 1967, in *BBC/ME*, 1 June and 28 September 1967.

11. *EH*, 30 September 1967; and Radio Addis Ababa, 6 and 8 November 1967, in *BBC/ME*, 8 and 10 November 1967.

12. See descriptions in Jack Kramer, "Hidden War in Eritrea," *Venture*, May 1969; and Karl Eric Knutsson, *Report from Eritrea* (Stockholm: IWGIA, 1971). See also an extensive interview with Abd al-Qadir Ramadan and Ahmad Muhammad Ibrahim in *al-Hadaf* (Beirut), 27 March 1971.

13. "A Political Report"; and EPLF, *National Democratic Program* (n.p., 31 January 1977).

14. "A Political Report."

15. Ibid.; and Lloyd Ellingson, "The Origins and Development of the Eritrean Liberation Movement," in Robert L. Hess, ed., *Proceedings of the Fifth International Conference on Ethiopian Studies* (Chicago, 1978, session B).

16. For details, see interview with Waldai Kassai in *EH*, 19 November 1967.

17. Haile Walda-Sellasse, "Man yemasker yanabara," *Addis Zaman*, 26 Maskaram 1972 EC.

18. "A Political Report."

19. Walda-Ab, "An Open Letter"; and "A Political Report."

20. Radio Damascus, 31 December 1968, in *BBC/ME*, 6 January 1968.

21. See *AC*, 27 November 1970; *al-Hadaf*, 27 March 1971; and *Domenica del Corriere*, 6 April 1971.

22. *Al-Hadaf*, 27 March 1971.

23. "A Political Report."

24. Ibid.; and *Domenica del Corriere*, 6 April 1971.

25. "A Political Report." See also *AC*, 27 November 1970; and *Domenica del Corriere*, 6 April 1971.

26. Pliny the Middle-Aged, "Eclectic Notes on the Eritrean Liberation Movement," *Ethiopianist Notes* 2, no. 1 (1978): 37–46.

27. For an example, see *al-Hayat* (Beirut), 5 June 1969; and Voice of the Fatah, 20 November 1969, in *BBC/ME*, 22 November 1969. Uthman's Arabic-language book on the history of Eritrea, however, reveals clearly that he is aware that Eritrean society has very little to do with Arabism.

28. *Eritrean Review* (Beirut?), June 1975.

29. See Voice of the Fatah, 20 November 1969, in *BBC/ME*, 22 November 1969; and "A Political Report."

30. *Al-Muharrir* (Beirut), December 1969.

31. "A Political Report."

32. Article by Uthman Sabi in *Filastin al-thawra* (Beirut), 19 September 1973.

33. For details, see *Africa Contemporary Record*, 1969/1970, pp. B111–12.

34. During the 1960s, Dr. Biasolo became the spiritual father of such youngsters as Isayas, Tedla Bairu's son Heruy Tedla, Fisseha Haragot (the son of the mayor of Asmara), Asmarom Amara (the nephew of Tesfa-Yohannes Berhe, the vice-governor of Eritrea throughout the 1960s), and other members of important Christian families who later became prominent in the Eritrean organizations. (In the late 1960s, Asmaron joined Uthman Sabi in Beirut, and Heruy went to the Sudan to join Idris Adam.)

35. See *AC*, 27 November 1970.

36. See the interview with Irmayas Debbasi in *Domenica del Corriere*, 23 March and 6 April 1971. By 1978 Irmayas was the spokesman for the EPLF in Rome.

37. *Domenica del Corriere*, 6 April 1971.

38. "A Political Report"; and *Domenica del Corriere*, 23 March and 6 April 1971.

39. Pliny the Middle-Aged, "Eclectic Notes," p. 38.

40. "A Political Report"; and Radio Damascus, 30 December 1970, in *BBC/ME*, 1 January 1971. (In August 1971 the General Union of Eritrean Students, affiliated with the ELF, was established in Baghdad. Students affiliated with the PLF formed their own body in Cairo at the same time.)

41. See Chapter 5; and *al-Hadaf*, 27 March 1971 (interview with leaders of the General Command).

42. See *al-Hadaf*, 27 March 1971; and *AC*, 27 November 1970.

43. "An Important Statement"—leaflet published in Beirut by the Eritrean Liberation Forces–Obel, dated 28 December 1971.

44. Radio Baghdad, 27 June 1971, in *BBC/ME*, 30 June 1971.

45. *Domenica del Corriere*, 23 March 1971.

46. See the resolutions of the ELF congress, Radio Damascus, 13 December 1971, in *BBC/ME*, 16 December 1971.

47. Pliny the Middle-Aged, "Eclectic Notes," p. 37.

48. For the resolutions of the ELF congress, see Radio Damascus, 6, 13, and 20 December 1971, in *BBC/ME*, 8, 16, and 23 December 1971; and *al-Ba'th* (Damascus), 8 January 1972.

49. "An Important Statement."

50. Haile Walda-Sellasse, "Man yemasker yanabara," *Addis Zaman*, 26 Makaram 1972 EC.

51. "Press Communique Issued by the Common Meeting Between the Eritrean Liberation Organs," Beirut, 13 February 1972, in *Africa Contemporary Record*, 1972/1973, p. C126.

52. Haile Walda-Sellasse, "Man yemasker yanabara," *Addis Zaman*, 26 Maskaram 1972 EC.

53. EPLF, *In Defense of the Revolution*, p. 137; and *Vanguard* (EPLF monthly), January 1973, pp. 5–6.

54. See descriptions in Haile Walda-Sellasse, "Man yemasker yanabara," *Addis Zaman*, 26, 28, and 29 Maskaram 1972 EC.

55. *Vanguard*, June 1976.

56. See Haile Walda-Sellasse, "Man yemasker yanabara," *Addis Zaman*, 28 Maskaram 1972 EC. Haile defected from the beaten and internally torn EPLF and joined the ELF-RC in November 1973.

57. *Sudanow* (Khartoum), April 1977.

58. *Ma'ariv* (Tel Aviv), 26 March 1974.

59. Paul B. Henze, an authority on both Soviet and Ethiopian affairs, believes that the key factor in Eritrea during the late 1960s and early 1970s was outside support. The radical Arabs who gave this support, he maintains, sometimes acted on their own—but more often than not their aims and intentions were essentially the same as those of the Soviets, with whom they were cooperating. A prime incentive with many of these people—both radical Arabs and Communists—was the conviction that they were injuring U.S. and Israeli interests by supporting Eritrea.

Chapter 3

1. See full text in Margery Perham, *The Government of Ethiopia*, 2d ed. (Evanston, Ill.: Northwestern University Press, 1969), p. 426.

2. Peter Schwab, *Decision-Making in Ethiopia* (London: C. Hurst, 1972), p. 53.

3. Christopher Clapham, *Haile Selassie's Government* (New York: Praeger, 1969), "Biographical Appendix." Clapham also provides a wealth of background information on Ethiopian politics during the late 1960s. For Asrate's role in the 1960 revolt, see Richard Greenfield, *Ethiopia: A New Political History* (New York: Praeger, 1965), pp. 395–98.

4. The administrative system and other relevant data were described in detail in a booklet published under the auspices of Asrate Kassa immediately after his appointment over Eritrea: Aradom Tedla, *Facts About Eritrea* (Asmara: n.p., 1964).

5. Both were *fitawraris* until 1966. When Asrate was made *ras* in 1966, he automatically obtained the authority to grant the title of *dadjazmach*.

6. See John Markakis, *Ethiopia: Anatomy of a Traditional Polity* (London: Oxford University Press, 1975), p. 366; and Jack Kramer, "Hidden War in Eritrea," *Venture*, May 1969.

7. According to Aradom Tedla, *Facts About Eritrea*, p. 20, in 1964 this police force numbered 4,378 men, under an Eritrean commissioner, Brig. Gen. Zara-Mariam Azazi. According to *Time*, 1 March 1971, the force numbered 5,000 men.

8. Mangasha Siyum was a great-grandson of Emperor Yohannes IV, the only Tigrean emperor in modern times. Mangasha had been governor of Tigre since 1961 and was the only provincial governor who was a member of a local family previously in power in the same province. In 1975 (after the revolution) *Ras* Mangasha became a founding member of the Ethiopian Democratic Union (see Chapter 6). Both Mangasha and Asrate were married to granddaughters of Haile Selassie, and both were rivals of Prime Minister Aklilu.

9. *WP*, 30 April 1962.

10. For a detailed description by the first European journalist to visit the territories occupied by the Eritrean organizations, see Franco Prattico, "Viaggio nell'Eritrea in Fiamme," *Paese Sera*, 9 May 1967 (also issued in Arabic by the ELF, *Rihla ila Irtriya al-mulhaba*).

11. See *WP*, 30 April 1967; *NYT*, 30 April 1967; and Radio Mogadishu, 14 March 1967, in *BBC/ME*, 16 March 1967.

12. *WP*, 30 April 1967.

13. See Chapter 5.

14. Radio Addis Ababa, 11 August 1967, in *BBC/ME*, 14 August 1967.

15. *NYT*, 27 August 1967.

16. See Chapter 2.

17. See Patrick Gilkes, *The Dying Lion* (New York: St. Martin's Press, 1975), p. 198. For details on military activities in the first half of 1968, see *Eritrea, New Bulletin*, 15 January 1968; Radio Damascus, 11 July 1968, in *BBC/ME*, 13 July 1968; and Kramer, "Hidden War in Eritrea."

18. For details, see Radio Damascus, 10 and 12 October 1968 and 23 January, 13 April, 14 June, and 6 September 1969, in *BBC/ME*, 12 and 15 October 1968 and 25 January, 15 April, 18 June, and 9 September 1969; *Africa Contemporary Record*, 1969/1970, p. B112; Gilkes, *The Dying Lion*, pp. 198–99; and Kramer, "Hidden War in Eritrea."

19. *AC*, 13 March 1970.

20. See ibid., 27 November 1970.

21. *Sunday Times*, 30 May 1971; and *Africa Contemporary Record*, 1971/1972, p. B113.

22. See *Daily Telegraph*, 30 December 1970.

23. See *Domenica del Corriere*, 6 April 1971.

24. Details in *Sunday Times*, 30 May 1971; and Karl Eric Knutsson, *Report from Eritrea* (Stockholm: IWGIA, 1971).

25. The upsurge of fighting in Eritrea that caused the Ethiopians so much strain and embarrassment in 1970—and resulted in the dismissal of Asrate Kassa—came to an end rather unexpectedly and in a manner much more favorable to Ethiopian interests than could have been anticipated. It was partly the result of hard effort and partly good luck—or, rather, bad luck on the part of the anti-Ethiopian interests. Haile Selassie's trip to Peking in December 1971 (accompanied by *Ras* Asrate) resulted in an agreement with the Chinese. In return for Ethiopian recognition, the Chinese agreed to

stop all support for the Eritrean rebel movement. The Chinese honored this agreement immediately. By the summer of 1972, Chinese support had stopped, and the intensity of Eritrean activity had lessened considerably. Moreover, the coup attempt of Sudanese Communists against Numayri in the summer of 1971—which came within a hair's breadth of succeeding—taught him a very important lesson about the Soviets. How much the Soviets were entangled in this whole process remains to be explained. Numayri, however, concluded that the Soviets had dealt dishonestly with him by permitting the coup to take place without warning him and proceeded to disengage. This was very difficult, for he had become militarily dependent on them. He wisely saw that the best way to reduce his military dependency was to remove the cause of such large military requirements—the rebellion in the southern Sudan. By this time it had become clear that the southerners could neither completely win nor decisively lose. They had had support from a good many outside sympathizers and players of the power game—including Israel and the United States. It was also clear that the Sudanese—in spite of massive Soviet aid and even direct Soviet involvement against the southerners—could neither win nor lose. The only sensible thing to do was to try to settle the whole business—Haile Selassie and other key Ethiopians were ready to help and were remarkably straightforward and efficient about doing it. By the end of 1971 the groundwork for the reconciliation, which was signed in February 1972, had been laid. In return, Sudanese tolerance for Eritrean support operations lessened, a situation that persisted until after the 1974 revolution.

26. An early 1971 statement by the information minister was typical: "Although it was possible that the ELF exists abroad, there was no organized action inside the province, only isolated incidents from time to time" (*Africa Diary* [New Delhi], 15–25 February 1971). For another example, see Radio Addis Ababa, 12 December 1972, in *BBC/ME*, 14 December 1972.

Chapter 4

1. For details, see U.S., Department of Defense, "Chronology of Ethiopian Affairs, 1 February–31 July 1974" (Washington, D.C.: Library of Congress, unpublished ms., 1974); and *Eritrean Review*, June 1974.

2. Haggai Erlich, "The Establishment of the Derg: The Turning of a Protest Movement into a Revolution," in Robert L. Hess, ed., *Proceedings of the Fifth International Conference on Ethiopian Studies* (Chicago, 1978), pp. 783–98.

3. *AC*, 22 March 1974.

4. See leaflet distributed in mid-May in Addis Ababa: "The Ethiopian People Will Not Be Frightened or Deterred by the Bad Deeds and Intrigues of *Leul Ras* Asrate Kassa."

5. U.S., Department of Defense, "Chronology of Ethiopian Affairs," pp. 7–8.

6. Ibid., pp. 8, 11, 14, 15.

7. Radio Addis Ababa, 18 July 1974, in *BBC/ME*, 20 July 1974.

8. "Ethiopia Tikdem," Declaration of the PMAC, Addis Ababa, 20 December 1974, p. 1.

9. Zawde Gabra-Sellasse [Zewde Gabre-Selassie], "Eritrea and Ethiopia in the Context of the Red Sea and Africa" (Washington, D.C.: Woodrow Wilson International Center, unpublished ms., 1976), p. 133.

10. See interview with Uthman Salih Sabi in *Eritrean Review*, June 1974.

11. U.S., Department of Defense, "Chronology of Ethiopian Affairs," p. 20.

12. *Financial Times (FT)*, 16 July 1974.

13. *Eritrean Review*, June 1974.

14. Radio Addis Ababa, 20 August 1974, in *BBC/ME*, 22 August 1974.

15. *Le Monde* (Paris), 26 November 1974.

16. See J. A. Kolmodin, *Traditions de Tsazzega et Hazzega: Textes Tigrigna*, 2 vols. (Rome: n.p., 1912, 1914); and Haggai Erlich, *Ethiopia and Eritrea During the Scramble for Africa: A Political Biography of Ras Alula* (Tel Aviv: Tel Aviv University, Shiloah Center; East Lansing: Michigan State University Press, 1982).

17. *International Herald Tribune (IHT)* and *FT*, 21 August 1974; and Radio Addis Ababa, 20 August 1974, in *BBC/ME*, 22 August 1974.

18. *Le Monde*, 26 November 1974.

19. *EH*, 28 August and 7 September 1974; and Radio Addis Ababa, 31 August 1974, in *BBC/ME*, 2 September 1974.

20. *EH*, 7 September 1974.

21. Gabra-Sellasse, "Eritrea and Ethiopia," p. 140.

22. *EH*, 7 September 1974; and Radio Addis Ababa, 24 September 1974, in *BBC/ME*, 26 September 1974.

23. *La Stampa* (Turin), 12 September 1974. See also *AC*, 19 December 1974.

24. *Eritrean Review*, September 1974, p. 4.

25. Ibid., p. 8.

26. According to another source (*AC*, 19 December 1974), a split already existed between the uncompromising Uthman Sabi and his EPLF colleagues in the field.

27. See the article by G. Roberts in *FT*, 28 October 1975. See also Haile Walda-Sellasse, "Man yemasker yanabara," *Addis Zaman*, 30 Maskaram 1972 EC.

28. See also Pliny the Middle-Aged, "Eclectic Notes on the Eritrean Liberation Movement," *Ethiopianist Notes* 2, no. 1 (1978), p. 39.

29. *Sudanow*, April 1977; and *FT*, 28 October 1975.

30. Radio Addis Ababa, 30 September 1974, in *BBC/ME*, 3 October 1974.

31. *EH*, 11 October 1974.

32. *Guardian*, 19 October 1974.

33. *Ma'ariv*, 21 October 1974.

34. *Africa Research Bulletin*, November 1974.

35. Radio Addis Ababa, 18 November 1974, in *BBC/ME*, 20 November 1974.

36. According to another version, he did try to mobilize support, but his aide-de-camp intercepted his telegrams and passed them to the Derg.

37. According to unconfirmed information, he was assassinated.

38. *NYT*, 3 February 1975.

39. *Guardian*, 24 December 1974.

40. *Times* (London), 24 December 1974.

41. *WP*, 28 December 1974.

42. *IHT*, 30 December 1974; and *Le Monde*, 4 January 1975.

43. *Jerusalem Post* (*JP*), 31 December 1974; *WP* and *FT*, 6 January 1975; *EH*, 7 January 1975; Radio Addis Ababa, 5 January 1975, in *BBC/ME*, 7 January 1975; and *NYT*, 3 February 1975.

44. *JP*, 16 January 1975; and *WP*, 23 February 1975.

45. Gabra-Sellasse, "Eritrea and Ethiopia," p. 146.

46. *Times* (London), 27 January 1975; and *Le Monde*, 30 January 1975.

Chapter 5

1. *Yediot Ahronot* (Tel Aviv), 23 June 1976; and *Ma'ariv*, 10 February 1978.

2. *Ma'ariv*, 10 February 1978.

3. Ibid., 9 February 1978.

4. *Yediot Ahronot*, 7 February 1978; and *Ma'ariv*, 8 February 1978.

5. Zawde Gabra-Sellasse [Zewde Gabre-Selassie], "Eritrea and Ethiopia in the Context of the Red Sea and Africa" (Washington, D.C.: Woodrow Wilson International Center, unpublished ms., 1976), p. 124; and Peter Schwab, "Israel's Weakened Position on the Horn of Africa," *New Outlook* 1978, no. 10 (April): 21–27.

6. The claim was that Israeli involvement in the area included a presence on some of the Dahlak islands just off the Eritrean coast near Massawa and armed occupation of Hanish and Zukar islands just north of the strait of Bab al-Mandab. Other sources mentioned the islands of Halib and Fatima. (See EPLF, *Zionist Presence in Eritrea* [n.p., 1970]; *al-Ba'th*, 18 January 1972; *Time*, 19 March 1973; and *Baltimore Sun*, 6 August 1970.)

7. See EPLF, *Zionist Presence in Eritrea*; "A Political Report"; *Standard* (Nairobi), 28 December 1970; and *Domenica del Corriere*, 6 April 1971. According to *Zionist Presence*, the first class of 300 Israeli-trained commandos at the Decamere base graduated in September 1964. By 1970, some 5,000 commandos had been trained there under the supervision of an Israeli colonel named Ben Natan.

8. From the diary of an Israeli officer and ex-adviser to the Ethiopian army.

9. In the spring of 1973, the Soviets supplied MiG-21s to the Somalis.

Ethiopian requests for equivalent planes were rejected by Washington. The emperor turned to Israeli Ambassador to Ethiopia Hannan Inor, and consequently the Israeli embassy in Washington persuaded President Nixon to reconsider the matter favorably. (See *Ma'ariv*, 10 February 1978.)

10. See also *Africa Contemporary Record*, 1973/1974, p. B161.

11. According to Zawde Gabra-Sellasse, this break made Haile Selassie senile. After the cabinet meeting at which the matter was settled, the emperor was never the same again. (Personal conversation with author, New York, 1978.)

12. Gabra-Sellasse, "Eritrea and Ethiopia," p. 119, quoting Muhammad Khalil, *The Arab States and the Arab League, Vol. 1, Constitutional Developments* (Beirut, 1962), p. 685.

13. See, for example, the map in *EH*, 4 September 1967.

14. *Standard*, 28 December 1970.

15. See *al-Anwar* (Beirut), 27 December 1970.

16. Gabra-Sellasse, "Eritrea and Ethiopia," p. 119.

17. *Observer*, 22 June 1969; and *EH*, 20 and 24 September 1967.

18. *Africa Contemporary Record*, 1973/1974, p. B155; Radio Baghdad, 1 October 1974, in *BBC/ME*, 3 October 1974; and *Ma'ariv*, 26 March 1974.

19. *Al-Muharrir*, 10 April 1969.

20. *Filastin al-thawra*, 19 September 1973.

21. *Al-Jumhuriyya* (Baghdad), 9 May 1969.

22. *Afro-Asian Affairs* (London), 14 February 1975.

23. *AC*, 13 March 1970.

24. Voice of the Fatah, 20 November 1969, in *BBC/ME*, 22 November 1969; see also the official statement by the PLO in *Eritrean Review*, September 1974.

25. See Uthman Sabi's speech, Radio Tripoli, 15 November 1970, in *BBC/ME*, 17 November 1970; and interview with Uthman in *Al-Fajr al-Jadid* (Tripoli), 24 April 1973.

26. See also *Ma'ariv*, 26 March 1974; and *Africa Contemporary Record*, 1973/1974, p. B155.

27. *Al-Hadaf*, 9 January 1971.

28. For the Ethiopian-Egyptian struggle over Eritrea during this period, consult Sven Rubenson, *The Survival of Ethiopian Independence* (London: Heinemann Educational Books, 1976); and Haggai Erlich, *Ethiopia and Eritrea During the Scramble for Africa: A Political Biography of Ras Alula* (Tel Aviv: Tel Aviv University, Shiloah Center; East Lansing: Michigan State University Press, 1982).

29. In November 1875 and March 1876, the Egyptians were beaten by Ethiopian Emperor Yohannes IV at Gundet and Gura, respectively.

30. Aluf Hareven, "The UAR in Africa" (Tel Aviv: Tel Aviv University, Shiloah Center, unpublished ms., 1962), p. 133.

31. *Afro-Asian Affairs*, 14 February 1975.

32. Radio Cairo, 7 November 1963, in *BBC/ME*, 8 November 1963.

33. *Afro-Asian Affairs*, 14 February 1975; In 1970 the number of Eritreans being trained in Algeria was estimated at 150 (*AC*, 13 March 1970).

34. *Ma'ariv*, 28 February 1967; *Christian Science Monitor* (*CSM*), 26 April 1967; and *Times* (London), 7 July 1967.

35. *Al-Ahram* (Cairo), 27 October 1972.

36. For the struggle between the Mahdist state of the Sudan and Ethiopia under the religious emperor Yohannes IV, culminating in the battle of Metemma on 9–10 March 1889, consult P. M. Holt, *The Mahdist State of the Sudan*, 2d ed. (London: Oxford University Press, 1970); Rubenson, *Survival*; Erlich, *Ethiopia and Eritrea*; and Zewde Gabre-Selassie, *Yohannes IV of Ethiopia* (London: Oxford University Press, 1975).

37. *AC*, 13 March 1970.

38. Jack Kramer, "Hidden War in Eritrea," *Venture*, May 1969, p. 21.

39. Radio Dar-es-Salaam, 17 October 1963, in *BBC/ME*, 19 October 1963; and Radio Mogadishu, 4 December 1964, in *BBC/ME*, 7 December 1964.

40. Radio Abidjan, 30 March 1964, in *BBC/ME*, 1 April 1964.

41. Radio Mogadishu, 28 January 1965, in *BBC/ME*, 30 January 1965.

42. *Africa Report*, April 1967.

43. *Africa Diary*, 9–15 July 1967.

44. See Middle East News Agency (MENA) dispatch, 30 May 1969, in *Itim Mizrah Broadcasts*, 31 May 1969; interview with Numayri in *al-Ahram*, 23 July 1969; and interview with Uthman Sabi in *al-Jarida* (Beirut), 25 June 1969.

45. *AC*, 18 December 1970.

46. Ibid.

47. *Times* (London), 7 and 12 April 1971.

48. In March 1973, following a Black September action in Khartoum, President Numayri charged that a Sudanese military patrol had been wiped out by ELF forces on the orders of a PLO leader (*Africa Contemporary Record*, 1973/1974, p. B155).

49. Gabra-Sellasse, "Eritrea and Ethiopia," p. 119.

50. Radio Mogadishu, 5 August 1965, in *BBC/ME*, 7 August 1965.

51. Radio Mogadishu, 2 May 1963, in *BBC/ME*, 4 May 1963.

52. *Observer*, 22 July 1969; Radio Addis Ababa (accusing Radio Mecca), 12 April 1963, in *BBC/ME*, 16 April 1963; and *Africa Diary*, 24–27 July 1962.

53. Radio Asmara, 8 January 1974, in *Eritrean Review*, February 1974.

54. *Africa* 16, no. 7 (11 April 1975).

55. *Al-Hayat*, 25 June 1969.

56. Even many Eritrean Muslims rejected Arabism as a component of Eritrean nationalism. See, for example, an interview with Muhammad Ahmad Abduh (the military commander of the ELF's General Command) in the Italian communist daily *L'Unità* (Rome), 15 February 1971.

57. See also Uthman Sabi in *al-Ray al-Amm* (Kuwait), 21 November 1972.

58. *Al-Gumhuriyya* (Cairo), 28 November 1974.

59. Ibid., 23 September 1974.

60. Radio Addis Ababa, 26 October 1974, in *BBC/ME*, 28 October 1974; and *EH*, 27 October 1974.

61. *Al-Nahar* (Beirut), 5 October 1974; *CSM*, 26 December 1974; *AC*, 19 December 1974; and *al-Hayat*, 2 December 1974.

62. Uthman Sabi in *al-Nahar*, 5 October 1974; and *Afro-Asian Affairs*, 28 February 1975.

63. Radio Kuwait, 16 February 1975.

64. See the interesting note in *NYT*, 25 February 1975.

65. *Ma'ariv*, 27 September 1974; *Africa Research Bulletin*, November 1974; and *AC*, 19 December 1974.

66. In December 1974 and January 1975, Ethiopia, fearing Arab military support for the separatists, sent two delegations to tour Arab capitals (see *FT*, 6 January 1975; and *Guardian*, 11 January 1975).

Chapter 6

1. *Observer*, 22 June 1969.

2. As usual, information about the number of casualties was one-sided and often exaggerated. The Derg claimed 2,321 rebels killed and 324 wounded, compared with 87 dead and 188 wounded for the Ethiopian army. Uthman Sabi's version was that 2,000 Ethiopian troops had been killed. (See *NYT*, 28 February 1975; and *Africa Report*, March 1975.)

3. *NYT*, 28 February 1975; *IHT*, 1–2 March 1975; and *JP*, 2 March 1975.

4. *Africa Report*, March–April 1975.

5. *NYT*, 3 and 22 February 1975; and *WP*, 7 February 1975.

6. *FT*, 26 May 1976; *NYT*, 19 May 1976; and Colin Legum and Bill Lee, *Conflict in the Horn of Africa* (London: Rex Collings, 1977), p. 35.

7. *WP*, 30 April 1977.

8. *JP*, 2 March 1975; *NYT*, 22 February 1975; and *WP*, 30 April and 14 May 1977. Legum and Lee, *Conflict in the Horn*, p. 59, puts the number for 1976 at 27,000.

9. *WP*, 20 May 1976; see also *CSM*, 28 February 1975.

10. See *AC*, 29 August 1975.

11. *NYT*, 12 May 1976.

12. See *Vanguard*, special issue, January 1976. Examples in *Liberation* (Eritreans for Liberation in North America), February–March 1975.

13. See communiqué issued by the EDU, 8 October 1975.

14. *EDU: What Does it Stand For* (London, 1976); and *EDU Advocate*, no. 2 (August 1976).

15. *Observer*, 12 October 1976; and *Guardian*, 3 October 1977.

16. *Sudanow*, April 1977; and *Sunday Times*, 12 December 1976.

17. EPLF, Foreign Mission, "Taqrir an al-awda' al-Ityopiyya," 16 June 1976; *Sunday Times*, 12 September 1976; and *Sudanow*, April 1977.

18. See *WP*, 26 June 1975.

19. *WP*, 14 May 1975; and *Vanguard*, January 1976.

20. See, for example, *WP*, 14 February and 14 May 1975; and UP dispatch, 17 February 1975.

21. *Vanguard*, January 1976.

22. See *AC*, 25 October 1975; and *Observer*, 2 March 1976.

23. The EPLF claimed some three thousand Ethiopian troops killed and a similar number wounded during 1975 (*Vanguard*, January 1976).

24. See *AC*, 7 January 1977.

25. EPLF, Foreign Mission, "Taqrir an al-awda'."

26. *NYT*, 12 May 1976.

27. Descriptions in EPLF, Foreign Mission, "Taqrir an al-awda'"; Legum and Lee, *Conflict in the Horn*, pp. 55–56; *NYT*, 12 and 19 May 1976; and *WP*, 19 May 1976.

28. See *WP*, 8 June 1976; *Guardian*, 29 June 1976; *Sunday Times*, 12 September 1976; EPLF, Foreign Mission, "Taqrir an al-awda'"; *Liberation*, November–December 1976; and Atnafu's speech, Radio Addis Ababa, 20 June 1976, in *BBC/ME*, 22 June 1976.

29. Before cancellation of the march, the United States issued a strong warning to the Derg to desist from pursuing a genocidal offensive in Eritrea. During the late spring of 1976, the Derg made elaborate preparations for dealing with the problems it anticipated would arise with world public opinion when it embarked on this march—some extremists wanted to kill or drive out most of the Eritrean population and repopulate the region with Ethiopians from the center and southern parts of the country. Word got out, and U.S. Secretary of State Henry Kissinger, who paid very little attention to Ethiopia at this time, sent a strong warning to the Derg. Not being able to feel assured of Soviet military support at this time, the Derg had to heed the U.S. warning. It was the last occasion when the United States intervened in Ethiopian affairs with any effect. Afterward, the political commotion in Addis Ababa led to a situation where it became impossible for the United States to continue its aid program—especially the supplying of ammunition and lethal weaponry—without some reservations. On the other hand, F-5Es had been delivered in April. The Derg—though some of its members clearly preferred a Soviet military relationship to continuation of the U.S. one—had to recognize that the U.S. relationship was still valuable.

30. *WP*, 20 June 1976.

31. See descriptions in *IHT*, 13 October 1976.

32. *Daily Telegraph*, 15 January 1977.

33. *WP*, 2 May 1977; and *Vanguard*, February–March 1977.

34. *Al-Sahafa* (Khartoum), 12 May 1977.

35. For detailed description, see *Vanguard*, August 1977.

36. See the interview with Ethiopian leaders, *JP*, 6 February 1977.

37. It is interesting to note that the core of the Ethiopian force then active in Bagemdir was a brigade of the 3rd Division shifted from the Ogaden Desert following Soviet assurances that Somalia was not planning an invasion.

Chapter 7

1. *Ma'ariv*, 4 March 1977. It is doubtful that anything came of this venture.

2. *Arab Post*, 26 February 1977, quoting *al-Fajr al-Jadid*.

3. *AC*, 29 August 1975.

4. *Sudanow*, February 1977.

5. Colin Legum and Bill Lee, *Conflict in the Horn of Africa* (London: Rex Collings, 1977), p. 67, and *al-Ba'th*, 14 January 1972.

6. *Sudanow*, February 1977.

7. *Al-Ray al-Amm*, 14 May 1977.

8. *Ibid.*

9. *Al-Hawadith* (Beirut), 6 May 1977.

10. *Al-Dustur* (Amman), 9 March 1977.

11. *Ma'ariv*, 4 March 1977.

12. *AC*, 7 January 1977.

13. *Al-Dustur*, 9 March 1977.

14. *Ma'ariv*, 4 March 1977.

15. *Ibid.*, 2 March 1977.

16. *Sudanow*, April 1977.

17. See *al-Ray al-Amm*, 14 May 1977.

18. *EH*, 26 and 29 April 1977.

19. *Ibid.*, 15 April 1977.

20. *Ibid.*, 2 May 1977.

21. *Al-Yaqza* (Kuwait), 2 May 1977; and *WP*, 30 April 1977.

22. *Al-Hawadith*, 6 May 1977.

23. *Guardian*, 10 August 1977.

Chapter 8

1. Reuters dispatch, Damascus, 25 June 1975.

2. *AC*, 25 October 1975.

3. Pliny the Middle-Aged, "Eclectic Notes on the Eritrean Liberation Movement," *Ethiopianist Notes* 2, no. 1 (1978): 39.

4. Haile Walda-Sellasse, "Man yemasker yanabara," *Addis Zaman*, 30 Maskaram 1972 EC.

5. For a list of RC members, see Pliny the Middle-Aged, "Eclectic Notes," p. 45.

6. See *FT*, 28 October 1975; and *AC*, 25 October 1975.

7. Haile Walda-Sellasse, "Man yemasker yanabara," *Addis Zaman*, 30 Maskaram 1972 EC.

8. For details, see ELF, *Political Program Approved by the 2nd National Congress of the ELF* (Liberated areas, 28 May 1975).

9. Ibid.; and *al-Nidal al-Irtiri*, 1 February 1976.

10. See *AC*, 19 December 1974.

11. Reuters dispatch, Addis Ababa, 3 July 1978.

12. For Uthman's views during this period, see Colin Legum and Bill Lee, *Conflict in the Horn of Africa* (London: Rex Collings, 1977), p. 58; and *al-Hawadith*, 6 May 1977.

13. *AC*, 29 August 1975.

14. Radio Baghdad, 8 September 1975, in *BBC/ME*, 19 September 1975; and Haile Walda-Sellasse, "Man yemasker yanabara," *Addis Zaman*, 30 Maskaram 1972 EC. (The chief mediator was the Iraqi Abu Ali, who had been active at the ELF-RC congress of May 1975.)

15. *Al-Nidal al-Irtiri*, 1 February 1976.

16. *AC*, 25 October 1975.

17. *Eritrean Revolution*, December 1975.

18. Legum and Lee, *Conflict in the Horn*, p. 58; and *WP*, 30 April 1977.

19. See *Liberation*, September and October 1976.

20. *Al-Nidal al-Irtiri*, 1 February 1976.

21. EPLF leaflet, 28 March 1976.

22. See EPLF, *In Defense of the Eritrean Revolution* (New York, 1978), especially pp. 140, 146–48.

23. *Liberation*, September and October 1976; and *Vanguard*, January 1976.

24. For details, see *Vanguard*, January 1976 and February and March 1977.

25. According to Patrick Gilkes (personal communication), Isayas was at the time taking insignificant sums of Saudi money.

26. *Al-Nidal al-Irtiri*, 1 February 1976.

27. *New Africa*, December 1977.

28. *Le Monde*, 11–12 December 1977.

29. *Sudanow*, April 1977.

30. *Vanguard*, February–March 1977, p. 23.

31. A list of their names can be found in Pliny the Middle-Aged, "Eclectic Notes," p. 46.

32. *Sudanow*, March 1977.

33. *Al-Tali'a* (Beirut), November 1977.

34. *Middle East*, March 1977.

35. EPLF, *In Defense of the Eritrean Revolution*.

36. For details, see *Sudanow*, April and May 1977.

37. Ibid., May 1977.

38. *WP*, 30 April 1977.

39. J. Randal in ibid.

40. *Al-Yaqza*, 2 May 1977.

41. *Al-Hawadith*, 6 May 1977.

42. *IHT*, 9 June 1976; and *FT*, 17 June 1976.

43. *Al-Dustur*, 19–25 November 1977; Arab News Agency (ANA) dispatch, 27 July 1977; and Legum and Lee, *Conflict in the Horn*, pp. 85–86.

44. For detailed information, see Haile Walda-Sellasse, "Man yemasker yanabara," *Addis Zaman*, 1–2 Teqemt 1972 EC.

45. Ibid.; and Pliny the Middle-Aged, "Eclectic Notes," p. 40.

46. *AC*, 4 and 18 November 1977; *Guardian*, 10 August 1977; and *al-Tali'a*, November 1977.

47. *Guardian*, 10 August 1977; and *al-Dustur*, 19–25 September 1977. See also Ibrahim Totil's accusations in Pliny the Middle-Aged, "Eclectic Notes," pp. 41, 43–44.

48. Radio Omdurman, 19 September 1977, in *BBC/ME*, 21 September 1977.

49. Radio Omdurman, 22 September 1977, in *BBC/ME*, 24 September 1977.

50. *Al-Tali'a*, November 1977.

51. *New African*, December 1977.

52. *Al-Tali'a*, November 1977; *AC*, 18 November 1977; *Eritrea in Struggle*, *Newsletter of the AESNA*, December 1977; and *New African*, December 1977.

53. *Al-Tali'a*, November 1977; AP dispatch, Rome, 27 December 1977; and *Eritrea in Struggle*, January 1978;

54. AP dispatch, Rome, 27 December 1977.

55. *JP*, 4 December 1977.

56. Reuters dispatch, Rome, 10 March 1978.

57. Ibid., 28 April 1978.

58. AP dispatch, Beirut, 6 May 1978.

59. Ibid., 28 July 1978.

Chapter 9

1. See, for example, a publication on the Zamacha campaign of sending students to rural areas: *Progress Report: Call of the Motherland* (Addis Ababa, August

1975), especially tables on p. 17. On the other hand, in early 1977 there were over a hundred urban associations in Asmara (*EH*, 20 April 1977).

2. See, for example, *EDU Advocate*, August 1976; and *EDU, Ethiopia: The State of the Nation* (September 1976).

3. More information on the program can be found in Marina Ottaway and David Ottaway, *Ethiopia: Empire in Revolution* (New York: Africana Publishing Co., 1978), pp. 120–23 and appendix.

4. Such a commission was formed in July 1976 (Radio Addis Ababa, 8 July 1976, in *BBC/ME*, 10 July 1976).

5. Radio Addis Ababa, 16 May 1976, in *BBC/ME*, 18 May 1976.

6. The ELF-RC has failed to recognize this reality. It is, in turn, blamed by the EPLF for the fact that the inhabitants of its sphere of control, such as many of the Afars and the Kunama tribesmen, are cooperating with the Ethiopian army.

7. *WP*, 18 February 1975; and Ottaway and Ottaway, *Ethiopia*, pp. 166–67.

8. Paradoxically, U.S. aid to Ethiopia during 1975 and 1976 quantitatively amounted to more than a third of the total aid given during the 1953–1977 period.

9. *WP*, 20 May and 12 June 1976; *Guardian*, 15 June 1976; EPLF, Foreign Mission, "Taqrir an al-awda' al-Ityopiyya," 16 June 1976; and Ottaway and Ottaway, *Ethiopia*, p. 160.

10. *Ma'ariv*, 9 February 1975.

11. EPLF, Foreign Mission, "Taqrir an al-awda'."

12. See, for example, *Ahbar al-alam al-islami*, 17 March 1975, quoting a book by Uthman Salih Sabi, *Al-Sira' hawl al-bahr al-ahmar* [The struggle over the Red Sea], p. 48.

13. EPLF, Foreign Mission, "Taqrir an al-awda'."

14. *Al-Hawadith*, 6 May 1977; and *Yediot Ahronot*, 2 October 1977.

15. Ottaway and Ottaway, *Ethiopia*, pp. 139–40.

16. See names and story in Radio Addis Ababa, 25 July 1976, in *BBC/ME*, 27 July 1976. See also *WP*, 26 July 1976; and *IHT*, 27 July 1976.

17. *Yediot Ahronot*, 14 July 1976; Radio Addis Ababa, 13 July 1976, in *BBC/ME*, 15 July 1976; *IHT*, 14 July 1976; and *CSM*, 15 July 1976.

18. For more on the EPRP, consult index in Ottaway and Ottaway, *Ethiopia*.

19. Ibid., p. 159; EPLF, Foreign Mission, "Taqrir an al-awda'"; *Tishrin* (Damascus), 13 December 1977; *AC*, 25 October 1975, 5 August 1977; and *Times* (London), 9 September 1977.

20. Pliny the Middle-Aged, "Eclectic Notes on the Eritrean Liberation Movement," *Ethiopianist Notes* 2, no. 1 (1978): 41.

21. Ottaway and Ottaway, *Ethiopia*, p. 141; and *AC*, 7 January 1973.

22. *AC*, 15 May 1977.

23. In the opinion of Paul B. Henze, an authority on both Soviet and Ethiopian affairs, Ethiopia had always been the real prize for the Soviets, but they could not reach for it prior to late 1977. It was for the purpose of getting themselves into

a better position to gain it that they had supported Eritrean separatism and the Somalis for so many years. When there were larger gains to be made, however, as there were in 1977, they exploited the opportunity without bothering too much about principles. I concur with this analysis. Yet this argument cannot be carried further—namely, that the Soviets are interested in a pro-Soviet Addis Ababa dominating the Horn. They rather prefer the Eritreans and the Somalis to be their clients too and remain a potential threat to Ethiopia, with the result that the Soviets, not Addis Ababa, will dominate the region.

24. *EH*, 6 May 1977; *IHT*, 6 May 1977; and *Ma'ariv*, 8 May 1977.

25. *EH*, 13 April 1977.

26. For a description by the first journalist to visit the camp, see Radio Budapest, 27 September 1977, in *BBC/ME*, 29 September 1977.

27. *AC*, 13 May 1977.

28. Ibid., 22 July, 5 August, and 9 September 1977.

29. *FT*, 26 August 1977; and *AC*, 9 September 1977.

Chapter 10

1. Reuters dispatch, London, 27 June 1978, quoting Radio Addis Ababa.

Glossary

Ato: Mister, title of respect.

Awraja: District, subprovince.

Dadjazmach: Honorary title of senior dignitaries, officials, and generals. Literally, "commander of the door." Not used officially since the revolution.

Derg: Committee. Popular name for Coordinating Committee of the Armed Forces, Police, and Territorial Army, which has led the revolution since June 1974.

Enderase: Representative; also deputy, vice-, regent.

Fitawrari: "General of the vanguard"; honorary title, just below *dadjazmach*.

Kifle hagar: Region. The post-revolutionary term for "province."

Lij: Prince, title of young noblemen; also, child, son.

Mareb Mellash: Territories beyond the Mareb. Medieval Ethiopian name for Eritrea.

Maridazmach: Ancient title of the sovereigns of Shoa. Restored by Haile Selassie and given to the crown prince only.

Naftanya: Rifleman, armed retainer, member of northern families settled in the south during its occupation by Menelik II.

Ras: The second highest title, just below that of *negus*.

Shamma: Toga-like garment.

Shifta: Bandit, highwayman, a person escaping the authority of his superiors.

Shum shir: Dismissal from office, reshuffling of offices.

Tsahafe te'zaz: "Scribe of orders," minister of the pen.

Taklay gezat: Province (abrogated after the revolution).

Select Bibliography

Abir, Mordecai. "The Contentious Horn of Africa." *Conflict Studies* 23 (June 1972): n.p.

Bell, J. Bowyer. "Eritrea: The Endemic Insurgency and International Order." *Orbis* 18 (Summer 1974): 427–50.

Campbell, John Franklin. "Rambling Along the Red Sea: The Eritrean Question." *African Affairs* 48 (1970): 537–48.

Checole, Kassahun. "Eritrea: A Preliminary Bibliography." *Africana Journal* 6 (1975): 303–14.

Clapham, Christopher. *Haile Selassie's Government.* New York: Praeger, 1969.

Conti Rossini, Carlo. *Principi di Diritto Conseutudinario dell'Eritrea.* Rome: Tipografia dell'Unione Editrice, 1916.

Cumming, D. C. "The Disposal of Eritrea." *Middle East Journal* 7, no. 1 (Winter 1953): 18–32.

Ellingson, Lloyd. "The Emergence of Political Parties in Eritrea, 1941–1950." *Journal of African History* 18 (1977): 261–81.

———. "The Origins and Development of the Eritrean Liberation Movement." In Robert L. Hess, ed., *Proceedings of the Fifth International Conference on Ethiopian Studies*, Chicago, 1978, session B.

Eritrean Liberation Front. *The Federal Case of Eritrea with Ethiopia.* Damascus, n.d.

Eritrean People's Liberation Front. *In Defense of the Eritrean Revolution.* New York, 1978.

———. *National Democratic Program.* N.p., 31 January 1977.

———. *Taqrir siyyasi an al-azma fi harakat tahrir Irtriya wata'sis quwat al-tahrir al-sha'-biyya* (Beirut, n.d. [1971?]).

———. *Zionist Presence in Eritrea.* N.p., 1970.

Erlich, Haggai. "1885 in Eritrea: The Year in Which the Dervistes Were Cut Down." *Asian and African Studies* 10 (1975): 281–322.

———. "The Eritrean Autonomy, 1952–1962: Its Failure and Contribution to Further Escalation." In Yoram Dinstein, ed., *Models of Autonomy*, New Brunswick, N.J.: Rutgers University Press, 1981, pp. 171–82.

———. "The Establishment of the Derg: The Turning of a Protest Movement into a

Revolution." In Robert L. Hess, ed., *Proceedings of the Fifth International Conference on Ethiopian Studies*, Chicago, 1978, pp. 783–98.

———. *Ethiopia and Eritrea During the Scramble for Africa: A Political Biography of Ras Alula*. Tel Aviv: Tel Aviv University, Shiloah Center; East Lansing: Michigan State University Press, 1982.

———. "'Tigrean Nationalism,' British Involvement and Haile-Sellasse's Emerging Absolutism: Northern Ethiopia, 1941–1943," *Asian and African Studies* 15, no. 1 (1982).

Farer, Tom J. *War Clouds on the Horn of Africa*. New York: Carnegie Endowment for International Peace, 1976.

Gabra-Sellasse, Zawde [Zewde Gabre-Selassie]. "Eritrea and Ethiopia in the Context of the Red Sea and Africa." Washington, D.C.: Woodrow Wilson International Center, unpublished manuscript, 1976.

———. *Yohannes IV of Ethiopia*. London: Oxford University Press, 1975.

Gershoni, Y. "The Relationship Between Italy-Eritrea-Ethiopia in the Years 1896–1935." Tel Aviv: Tel Aviv University, M.A. thesis, 1976.

Gilkes, Patrick. *The Dying Lion*. New York: St. Martin's Press, 1975.

Great Britain. War Office. "Military Report on Eritrea." London: Public Record Office, PRO, WO 33/410, n.d. [1909?].

Greenfield, Richard. *Ethiopia: A New Political History*. New York: Praeger, 1965.

Habte-Selassie, Bereket. *Conflict and Intervention in the Horn of Africa*. New York: Monthly Review Press, 1980.

Hareven, Aluf. "The UAR in Africa." Tel Aviv: Tel Aviv University, Shiloah Center, unpublished manuscript, 1962.

Holt, P. M. *The Mahdist State of the Sudan*. 2d ed. London: Oxford University Press, 1970.

Knutsson, Karl Eric. *Report from Eritrea*. Stockholm: IWGIA, 1971.

Kolmodin, J. A. *Traditions de Tsazzega at Hazzega: Textes Tigrigna*. 2 vols. Rome: n.p., 1912, 1914.

Kramer, Jack. "Hidden War in Eritrea." *Venture*, May 1969.

Legum, Colin. *Ethiopia: The Fall of Haile Selassie's Empire*. London: Rex Collings, 1975.

Legum, Colin, and Lee, Bill. *Conflict in the Horn of Africa*. London: Rex Collings, 1977.

Loban, Richard. "The Eritrean War: Issues and Implications." *Canadian Journal of African Studies* 10 (1976): 335–46.

Longrigg, Stephen Hemsley. *A Short History of Ethiopia*. Oxford: Clarendon Press, 1945.

Luther, Ernest W. *Ethiopia Today*. Stanford: Stanford University Press, 1958.

Markakis, John. *Ethiopia: Anatomy of a Traditional Polity*. London: Oxford University Press, 1975.

Nadel, S. F. "Land Tenure of the Eritrean Plateau." *Africa* 16 (1946): 1–22, 99–109.

Ottaway, Marina, and Ottaway, David. *Ethiopia: Empire in Revolution*. New York: Africana Publishing Co., 1978.

Pankhurst, Estelle Sylvia, and Pankhurst, Richard. *Ethiopia and Eritrea: The Last Phase of the Reunion Struggle, 1941–1952*. Woodford Green, Eng.: Lalibela House, 1953.

Perham, Margery. *The Government of Ethiopia*. 2d ed. Evanston, Ill.: Northwestern University Press, 1969.

Perini, Ruffillo. *Di Qua Dal Mareb*. Florence: Tipografia Cooperative, 1905.

Pliny the Middle-Aged. "Eclectic Notes on the Eritrean Liberation Movement." *Ethiopianist Notes* 2, no. 1 (1978): 37–46.

Rubenson, Sven. *The Survival of Ethiopian Independence*. London: Heinemann Educational Books, 1976.

Schiller, Arthur A. "Eritrea: Constitution and Federation with Ethiopia." *American Journal of Comparative Law* 2 (1953): 375–83.

Schwab, Peter. *Decision-Making in Ethiopia*. London: C. Hurst, 1972.

———. "Israel's Weakened Position on the Horn of Africa." *New Outlook* 1978, no. 10 (April): 21–27.

Tamrat, Tadesse. *Church and State in Ethiopia, 1270–1527*. London: Oxford University Press, 1972.

Tedla, Aradom. *Facts About Eritrea*. Asmara: n.p., 1964.

Trevaskis, Gerald Kennedy Nicholas. *Eritrea: A Colony in Transition, 1941–1952*. London: Oxford University Press, 1960.

Trimingham, John Spencer. *Islam in Ethiopia*. London: Oxford University Press, 1962.

Ullendorff, Edward. *The Ethiopians: An Introduction to Country and People*. London: Oxford University Press, 1960.

———. trans. and annotator. *The Autobiography of Emperor Haile Selassie I, 1892–1937*. London: Oxford University Press, 1976.

United Nations. General Assembly. *Official Records, 7th Session: Supplement no. 15*. 1952.

United States. Department of Defense. "Chronology of Ethiopian Affairs, 1 February–31 July 1974." Washington, D.C.: Library of Congress, unpublished manuscript, 1974.

Uthman Salih Sabi [Othman Saleh Sabi]. *The History of Eritrea*. Trans. by Muhammad Fawaz al-Azem. Beirut, n.d. (1974).

Vigo, Anthony. "Between Two Worlds." *Africa Today*, October 1965, pp. 6–8.

Index